The Way of Truth
to a Life of Wholeness

TRACI LAWRENCE

Traci Lawrence

CROSSBOOKS
PUBLISHING

CrossBooks™
A Division of LifeWay
1663 Liberty Drive
Bloomington, IN 47403
www.crossbooks.com
Phone: 1-866-879-0502

First published by CrossBooks 7/24/2013

ISBN: 978-1-4627-2886-2 (sc)
ISBN: 978-1-4627-2888-6 (hc)
ISBN: 978-1-4627-2887-9 (e)

Library of Congress Control Number: 2013910517

Printed in the United States of America.

This book is printed on acid-free paper.

Table of Contents

Acknowledgements

The completion of this book is the result of a multitude of deposits made into my life by many people and many events, all of which were chosen or allowed by my Heavenly Father. There is no way to possibly know or make mention of all of these sources of help, encouragement and correction, but it is important to recognize and graciously thank those that I am aware of.

God, He is my: Maker, Father, Sustainer, Protector, Provider, Hope, Joy, Peace, Strength, Friend, Forgiveness and Encourager. He is my life and my everything. He held on to me when I deserved to be dropped, He provided freedom when I deserved prison; He gave me eternal life when all I could earn was death. My deep desire is for my life mission to one day abide by the verse found in John 4:34, "My food is to do the will of Him who sent me, and to finish His work"

My husband, who is my best, dearest and most preferred human friend on this earth. You have shown me a love, support, kindness and compassion that can only come from someone who walks with God. You were brought to me as a beautiful gift from God to help me on this difficult journey of life. You have shown encouragement, patience, laughter and generosity to me everyday of our lives together. You are the most free and beautiful person I have ever known. May our years together allow me the opportunity to give back all you have given me.

My parents, they are my foundation builders. Daily I thank God for giving you as my parents. You always provided for all my needs even if that meant your own were not met. You taught me about helping those who were hungry, or those whose car broke down or those who didn't have a coat to wear. You stressed upon me the importance of standing for justice and helping those who are too weak to help themselves. You provided a safe home and exposed me to the most important truth, God.

My children, these precious people allowed me to grow up beside them. They helped me see what is really important in life.

My Sunday school class, this is the class I have searched for my whole adult life.

Dr. Steve Wilson, my awesome Sunday school teacher who every Sunday displays the ability to balance fun, solid Biblical facts, humility and complete dedication to teaching the word of God.

Dr. Dan Summerlin, he is the Senior Pastor of Lone Oak First Baptist Church. His encouragement to write a book is what prompted me to pull a neglected manuscript out of the drawer and finish it. His teaching and faithful Shepherding help to feed me and my family on a regular basis.

My Oppositions, whether they be people or events. "But as for you, you meant evil against me, but God meant it for good, in order to bring it about as it is this day, to save many people alive" (Genesis 50:20).

Introduction

JESUS IS THE ANSWER!

The experience ushered in by 20 years of working bi-vocationally in the fields of mental health/social services and health/physical fitness have provided a tremendous learning and growing experience. These years combined with my own personal struggle with a life-controlling issue, a very short one year marriage to an abusive man and then a 12 year long marriage to an alcoholic, have confirmed that we all are wounded or lacking at some point in our lives and that Jesus is the answer, He is the only true and eternal answer to our wholeness. Unfortunately too few people actually seek this true source of wholeness; hence many continue to live in want, lack and brokenness. Without Jesus all our human attempts are short-lived success at best.

I was blessed with the opportunity to found a shelter for women and children who are homeless or victims of abuse. It was amazing to watch as God performed a miracle in building this organization from nothing. No money. No land. No building. No large community or group support. No advanced degree and No experience at organizational development. The miracle was not so much in the funding resources He provided because God owns it all. The miracle was that He used me, a messed-up, doubting, angry, foolish, confused and poor young woman, with a bad mouth (at that time). One thing I did have in my favor was the possibility that the old saying "we learn from our mistakes," might be true. If it is true then I should be a stinking genius.

My experiences as Director at the shelter and my second job as a personal trainer allowed me to work with populations that seemed to be at extremes. At the shelter, I worked with victims of physical and sexual abuse, extreme poverty, homelessness, severe depression, hopelessness, alcoholism and other drug addictions. On a regular basis I worked with people who had no place to call home and literally didn't have a penny to their name, or hopes of getting one anytime soon.

Each day after working with people who were living in desperate and heart breaking situations, I would go to the gym and work with my personal training clients. This clientele provided a different view from a different population. Those individuals seeking my services as a personal trainer mostly consisted of men and women who were typically wealthy, highly accomplished and appeared to have it all together, in fact many of them made more in a week than I made in a year. People in this group, in spite of their outward appearances of success, were also in need and experienced lack or weakness in one or more areas of their lives.

The women at the shelter were in severe lack of financial resources, and usually lacking in education, social support and suffering poor health. The Personal training clients, on the other hand were financially well off, but struggled with social wellness and their relationships, they very frequently had poor health and dealt with the consequences of pursuing money rather than developing their health and relationships. Both groups struggled with some type of unhealthy mental/emotional issues and their spiritual wellbeing was ignored and very weak.

Whether we are dealing with a severe lifestyle disease, financial crisis or struggling with a life controlling issue, it's important to know that we didn't arrive at this point in our life just because of one or two bad decisions, these struggles are the result of a lifestyle of unhealthy or ungodly decisions. These decisions are often the result of extreme fear, pain, confusion, deceit or shame. Sometimes they are due to lack of guidance, love and support or often times from a lack of knowledge. In some cases our bad decisions can be the result of pride and false self sufficiency or self righteousness.

Regardless of past events and mistakes or painful childhoods, it is now time for all of us to realize that the decisions we make in the present are ours to make and we CAN make Godly (healthy) decisions. "For God has not given us a spirit of fear, but of power and of love and of a sound mind" (2 Timothy 1:14). He gave us: power, love and a sound mind. These are tools, and when combined with the truth and knowledge found in the word of God they are powerful and life changing.

Tools and knowledge are necessary and very beneficial, but no matter how powerful the tools or how much knowledge we acquire, these tools and knowledge will be useless if we don't put them to use, and we must put them to use on a daily basis, day after day. Wholeness is a process and it actually never ends because it results from engaging in a God driven lifestyle….for life.

Each of us will have areas in ours life that are strong or more developed than others, this is great, we should genuinely thank God for this and celebrate the victory. Then we need to find someone who is struggling in the area where we are strong and become their mentor, and help them on their journey to wholeness. This action is actually a sign of social wellness, which will be covered in more detail a little later. It is also a great way to imitate Christ.

The ability to develop and enjoy wholeness comes from consistently adhering to a God driven lifestyle, which is also a healthy lifestyle. No one can live this life style for you. You may have the finances to pay someone to exercise and eat right but, it only benefits you if YOU do the exercising and eating right. You might have every tool ever designed, they are only functional if picked up and used for their intended purpose.

Ultimately our wholeness is based on our choices and actions. Those from our past, those we make right now, and the ones we will make and take in our future. If we want a good life, the abundant life that Jesus came to give, then it is up to each of us to build it. No one can do it for us, and if we will seek, obey and trust in God, then no one can stop us either.

Before starting this book, I wanted to write something that would be useful to Christians and non-Christians. I believe that regardless of personal beliefs this book can be useful to everyone, because it is based on the word of God, and the word of God is the ultimate hand book for life, authored by the Giver of life. This book will also be beneficial because each of us has room for improvement and all of us need to learn to walk in victory and live a life of wholeness. We all have a body, a mind, and a spirit, along with financial needs and social needs and responsibilities.

Christians are those who have asked Jesus into their hearts (This process is described in chapter 1). This group of people has believed in and accepted the greatest truth in the history of the world. Unfortunately many in this group fail to tell this and many more fail to live it. The lost world often sees the choices and lifestyles of Christians, and they want nothing to do with this God we speak about. Every component of our lives should reflect Christ. Unfortunately they don't.

Look at and consider the quote originally made by American author, friar, priest and speaker, Brennan Manning (April 27, 1934) "*The number one cause of Atheism is Christians, they acknowledge Jesus with their lips, but they walk out the door and deny Him with their lifestyle, this is what an unbelieving world finds unbelievable.*"

The first time I heard this it broke my heart and it still breaks my heart and convicts me. What sets us apart? Do we demonstrate the love of God on a regular basis? Do we obey His word, or do we live, act, talk and think like the world?

All believers are called to be ministers. It might not be at a pulpit or on the mission field in Africa, but each of us are to be ministers of God's word. Our world is hurting, lost, confused, angry and rebellious. We have the answer! Now it is up to us to share it, not only in our words but in our deeds.

For those who have invited Christ into your life, I pray this book will help you see and receive the wholeness that God offers, and then put it to use in our world to help build His kingdom. God has expectations for His children.

If you do not currently have a personal relationship with Jesus Christ, please read Chapter 1. With that chapter is a special message to non-believers. It will not be a waste of time. It will be an investment in your future and hopefully lead you to make the most important decision you will ever make. God has touched my life, He has blessed me, forgiven, and healed me. I want everyone to know and experience the hope, healing, comfort, love, peace, forgiveness and wholeness that God offers.

PART 1

WHAT IS WHOLENESS
AND
WHY IS IT IMPORTANT?

Chapter 1

A SPECIAL MESSAGE TO NON-BELIEVERS

If you have picked this book up or someone has given it to you and, you are struggling with your belief in Christ, don't put the book down yet. Read it. Your time will not be wasted. Yes, I do want you to come to know and trust God, but that is your decision 100 percent. God will not force Himself on you and, I'm not trying to force my beliefs on you either. I am merely trying to share His truth and the greatest source of hope and strength I know.

Wholeness is a beautiful gift of God, and it can only be fully obtained and enjoyed through a personal relationship with God. No amount of human effort, intelligence or riches can provide this treasure to us.

I want to share an answer to your problems, whatever they are or how many you may be struggling with. I want to offer suggestions to help you on life's long and sometimes painful journey.

I want to let you know that, God loved you so much that He gave His only son to pay for your sin so you could live with Him for eternity. "For God so loved the world that he gave His only begotten Son, that whoever believes in Him should not perish but have everlasting life" (John 3:16).

I want you to take comfort in what Psalm 27:10 says, "When my father and my mother forsake me the Lord will take care of me." I also want you to know that God has a plan and purpose for you. Jeremiah 29:11 states, "For I know the thoughts that I think toward you, says the Lord, thoughts of peace and not of evil, to give you a future and a hope." My prayer is that this book will help you desire to seek and know God and can help you begin your journey towards wholeness.

If you have never had a trust or belief in God, perhaps your un-belief comes from a life of many years living with people who lied to you, used you, abused you or humiliated you. Their actions were wrong. They were following their own selfish desires. These desires stem from their own pain, fear, confusion or erroneous beliefs. Their actions and desires were not God given.

Possibly your unbelief of what the Bible says is due to the fact that you have been hurt or led astray by someone professing to be a Christian. Yes, there are hypocrites in the world. In fact, aren't we all guilty of this to some degree? We all make attempts to look good in public and try our best to impress others, yet in the secret dark places of our lives we often struggle with and commit the same sins we are judging others for. If this is the case, take the time to read the entire book and see what God really expects of those who are His followers. Many of His children fail and at some point all of His children have disobeyed Him. The hope is that through these failures the products of wisdom, empathy and genuine repentance would result.

Please don't judge our heavenly Father by our failures, sin and shortcomings. People can really make God look bad. Many speak the Word when it benefits them but fail to live it. Those who are followers of Christ are just works in progress; they have by no means "arrived". I implore you to get to know God on your own. He really wants you to come to Him; He is just waiting for you.

Keep in mind that initially the only difference in Christians and non-Christians is that the Christians know they need God and have asked Him into their lives. In time however, there should be evident works in the life of a Christian to show that they are drawing closer to and becoming more like their heavenly Father.

Christians are not perfect, although I have met a few who seem to think they are. They are just forgiven. They are forgiven because of what Jesus did on the cross, not because of anything special or great they have done. Jesus was the Son of God. He willingly took on the physical limitations of a physical body and lived on this earth among people. Jesus gave His life on the cross to pay for the sin of the world, and provide forgiveness. This forgiveness is available to anyone who believes, calls upon the name of the Lord, confesses their sin and asks Jesus to come into their heart to be their Savior. "That if you confess with your mouth the Lord Jesus and believe in your heart that God has raised Him from the dead, you will be saved" (Romans 10:9).

Jesus died on the cross for everyone. He has paid the price in full. Now, He is waiting for you to ask and receive.

There are many references to the Bible in this book. This is because the Word of God is truth and is an absolute essential for personal wholeness. I ask you to consider one thing, whether you are a believer or not. What if everyone in the world knew and obeyed the principles listed in the word of God? If each of us would at a minimum just apply the 10 commandments to our lives no one would be hurting, angry, abused, fearful, confused or hungry....or lost. But many people refuse to do this. We are now seeing and living the results of this refusal.

Dear reader, please take the time to get to know God, not just know about Him, but really know Him; the one who died to pay for all of our sins.

There is nothing too bad for God to forgive. There is nothing you have done that is so awful that will keep Him from loving you. There is no addiction so strong that His power cannot deliver you from. He is just waiting on you. What are you waiting for? What else in this world promises you unconditional love? What else is always truth? When will you draw your last breath? Why turn away the greatest gift ever given? All these things are available to those who call upon the name of the Lord.

This is your personal choice. This choice will have ramifications for your eternity and for those who have or who will have a relationship with you. Do you want to help make the world a better place? Then seek God and accept Him into your life. Watch what He can do with a willing and seeking heart. The decision to ask God into your life will be the absolute best and most important decision you will ever make. I promise!

Take a moment right now and hear me say that Jesus died on the cross to forgive all of our horrible sins. It is hard to believe, but God will even help you with your unbelief if you ask Him. Accept what Jesus did for you and invite Him to come into your life and be your savior.

After you have asked Jesus into your life, get your own personal Bible and make it a point to spend time reading about and talking to God everyday. He really wants to hear from you and reveal Himself to you.

The process of salvation and accepting Jesus into your life is simple and requires only a honest and seeking heart and a genuine recognition of our sinfulness and need for a Savior. Make your desire for forgiveness known to Jesus right now.

The Bible tells us:

- "For all have sinned and fall short of the glory of God" (Romans 3:23).
- "The wages of sin are death, but the gift of God is eternal life through Jesus Christ our Lord" (Romans 6:23).

    Everyone has sinned. All of us!

Jesus died to pay the price for our sins

—"For God so loved the world that he gave his only begotten son, that who so ever believes in Him should not perish but have everlasting life" (John 3:16).

—"But God demonstrates His own love towards us, in that while we were still sinners, Christ died for us" (Romans 5:8).

Don't read over that too quickly, if you do you might miss the part that says; *while we were still sinners.* Jesus didn't wait until we quit lying, overcame our addictions, became loyal spouses, good parents or honest at our jobs. He died while we were messed up. He knew that was the only way to restore us.

—"For He made Him who knew no sin to be sin for us, that we may be made the righteousness of God in Him" (II Corinthians 5:21).

Jesus <u>willingly</u> gave His life as a sacrifice to pay for all of human sin.

<u>Believe and then ask Jesus into your heart</u>

—"that if you confess with your mouth the Lord Jesus and believe in your heart that God has raised Him from the dead, you will be saved; for with the heart one believes unto righteousness, and with the mouth confession is made unto salvation" (Romans 10:9-10).

—"For whoever calls upon the name of the Lord shall be saved" (Romans 10:13).

Make your desire for forgiveness and eternal life in heaven known to Jesus right now by praying and telling Him this. Confess your sins and ask him into your life. Don't wait another day.

Chapter 2

—•⇒•—

A SPECIAL MESSAGE TO CHRISTIANS

Eighteenth century political speaker, Edmund Burke (January 12, 1729–July 9, 1797) made the statement that all of us have seen or heard many times, *"Evil prospers when good men do nothing."* This is a wise and very true observation. When we look at the sinfulness of our world we shouldn't be surprised when the non-saved and non-believing engage in corruption, adultery, fraud, murder, abuse, deceit and extortion. This is behavior that is a characteristic of non-believers; they are following the father of lies. The problem is that we as believers don't display behaviors that should be characteristic of Christians; we don't follow our Father, the creator of Heaven and Earth.

What stops us from being salt & light? What hinders us from treating others as Christ did? What prevents us from spreading the good news of the Gospel? Why are we keeping the answer to any and every problem to ourselves? Why do Christians remain silent in the face of corruption and perversion when the lost world boldly promotes their wicked beliefs?

We as Christians can be deceived because we often fall prey to selfish desires. Sometimes, followers of Christ can let fear rule our thoughts and actions, or allow pride and arrogance to make us content, comfortable and blind to our own sin. Christians are humans with limitations, and humans do get tired and lose hope from relying on their own strength. Christians must acknowledge that once we are saved or born again, our journey towards wholeness has just begun. It means we have asked Jesus into our hearts and we have become new. 2 Corinthians 5:17 tells us, "Therefore, if anyone is in Christ, he is a new creation; old things have passed away; behold, all things have become new." This is all because of what Jesus did. The difference in us is Christ! Now, we have become His and we are to be a light in the darkness.

Since Christ is in us, it is important to know and believe, *there is a difference;* that we have been made more than conquerors. This is confirmed in Romans 8:37, "Yet in all these things we are more than conquerors through Him who loved us." Not through our intelligence, financial prosperity, strength or hard work. But through Him who loved us. Many of us probably have heard this verse, some may have even memorized it, but do we believe it? If we say we believe it but don't live it, do we really believe it? I will be asking this question again.

What is stopping us from celebrating and walking in the victory that Christ has already secured for us? Why do our personal, financial, social and business choices often seem to be more similar to those choices of the lost world than they are to the ones God desires for us?

People are watching Christians. Unfortunately our actions speak louder than our words. Perhaps we should follow a quote made famous by St. Francis of Assisi (1181/1182—Oct.3, 1226) *"Preach the gospel everyday, if necessary use words."* Our everyday choices, that we live out for everyone to see, are the avenues that God can use to reach a lost world. All of us must commit to the practical application of God's word to every part of our lives.

Every follower of Christ has been called into the ministry of reconciliation, the reconciliation of creation to its Creator. There are a multitude of branches that make up this ministry and every one of them serves an important and needed function. This is not just for those who are working full-time serving on a Church staff or in the mission fields, every child of God has a calling.

Sometimes this calling or ministry is hard work. My very wise pastor, Dr. Dan Summerlin, once said; "Ministry can drain the soul out of you." I have heard many people in ministry, and I myself have said someone needs to start a ministry for ministers. My prayer and intent is to help provide a form of that. I want to assist and encourage the children of God, my brothers and sisters in Christ, on their journey towards wholeness. Jesus desires this for His followers and He expressed it in John 10:10, "I have come so that they may have life, and that they may have it more abundantly."

The intention of this book is not merely for self-improvement, although learning and applying the word of God to our lives will definitely improve them. It is offered to assist, minister to, encourage, nurture and equip the saints, in line with Ephesians 4:12, "For the equipping of the saints, for the work of ministry, for the edifying of the body of Christ." This edifying (building up) is ultimately to help us minister to and tell a hurting world about Christ.

Ministering and meeting needs often require action on our part. Think about some of the things Jesus commands us: Go, tell, help, support, give, feed, plant, harvest, work, all of these are verbs, they are action words. If we are to effectively do these things we need to strengthen our minds, bodies, spirits, finances and relationships. Each of us needs healing, correction, encouragement, protection, strength and nourishment. We are fighting a battle and we are soldiers for Christ. Stop and consider how much time, effort, and money the U.S. Government allocates annually to the training and preparation of its soldiers. Shouldn't we the body of Christ do as much?

When the body of Christ is trained, equipped, built up, and sold out for Jesus, we are more effective at reaching a lost world for Christ. God blesses us so that we can be a blessing to others. These blessings can come in many forms, not just financial. They are given to us to use on His behalf to reach a lost world. The amount of power and blessings God gives His children is directly related to His children's willingness to use it on His behalf. "Most assuredly, I say to you, he who believes in Me, the works that I do he will do also; and greater works than these he will he do, because I go to my Father"(John 14:12).

Dear co-servant, we have the answer regardless of the problem. We have the truth and that truth leads to life. We are wrong and we are disobeying our Heavenly Father when we don't share the truth, love, grace, compassion, mercy and forgiveness that God so freely shared with us. The wholeness that God wants to develop in us will be the tool we use to reach and tell the world about our loving Father.

Stop here before going to the next chapter and ask our Father to make you aware of and sensitive to the human hurts and needs around you. Ask Him also, to help you discover your own personal needs, scars, fears and unhealthy habits that may be preventing you from developing your personal wholeness in Jesus. Thank Him that wholeness is possible through Him, and thank Him that He desires for you to enjoy it and He wants to help you develop it. Wholeness starts with Jesus, it is not possible without Him.

Chapter 3

WHAT IS WHOLENESS?

Often we hear the words wellness and wholeness interchanged, and typically when hearing one of these words *wellness,* people tend to think mostly of living healthy and disease free or eating right and exercising. This is partially correct but, physical health is only one component of wholeness. When we focus exclusively on physical health and ignore our whole being we are in for eventual problems that could be avoided. Ultimately our wholeness starts with God. It is from God, of God, through God and for God.

When hearing the term wholeness I want you to consider two different verses. The first is found in II Corinthians 9:8. "And God is able to make all grace abound towards you, that you, always having all sufficiency in all things, may have an abundance for every good work." The most important part of that verse is the first four words; *And God is able.*—So first our wholeness starts with God!

Next, listen to the times the word all or one of its synonyms is used:

1. <u>All grace</u>—Not just some grace or a little bit of grace...but all grace. How many of us need grace? We all do, in fact we need it every day...several times a day. Notice in that same sentence that in addition to providing all grace He also makes it abound towards us. That first part of the verse alone is enough...and God is able to make all grace abound.

2. <u>Always having</u>—This means all the time, not just Monday—Friday from 9-5. It means morning, noon and night. It means it is available

13

24 hours a day, 7 days a week, 52 weeks per year, for eternity. It is always available to us, because He is always with us.

3. <u>All sufficiency</u>—This means enough to meet one's needs, satisfactory, all you need, adequate. Just in case the words all and sufficiency don't comfort and reassure us, He puts them together and, instead of a double negative, which is improper in the English language, God puts them together as a double positive. This causes the meaning of the words to be strengthened and emphasized. God knows His children can be a little dense at times.

4. <u>All things</u>—Once more all is used in regards to things, this means everything! I know I might be making this sound redundant, but all these *alls* are really in this verse. God is really trying to let His children know that He has it all covered. *All things* includes our financial situations, our physical health, our relationship, our jobs, our mental and emotional wellness and our Spiritual health. Our wholeness.

5. <u>Have an abundance</u>—We all know what abundance means. This is just one more display of Gods patience towards His children. He wants to make sure we have got this. He is lacking in nothing.

6. <u>Every good work</u>—Look at the last phrase. I think it is included just in case we start to get selfish or prideful. God knows us very well doesn't He? We are reminded here why God provides for our wholeness. It is for every good work. We are blessed and have access to the love, power and resources of God so that we in turn will have everything that we need to work on His behalf.

The second verse that describes wholeness is found in Isaiah 9:6, "For unto us a Child is born, unto us a Son is given; and the government will be upon His shoulder. And His name will be called Wonderful, Counselor, Mighty God, Everlasting Father, Prince of Peace." Look at everything this verse tells He is. He is everything, He is our all in all.

Consider though specifically the phrase "Prince of Peace". Peace is often how we describe the word "shalom." According to Strong's concordance 7965, shalom means completeness, wholeness, health, welfare, safety, soundness, tranquility, prosperity, perfectness, fullness, rest, harmony, the absence of agitation or discord. Review those words once more, they each describe wholeness and they are each also speaking of Jesus.

It might sound a bit simple but, an easy way to describe wholeness is; **knowing God**….not just knowing about Him, but truly and deeply knowing and trusting in His wonderful, powerful, loving, patient, trustworthy, gentle, merciful, compassionate, generous and magnificent character. Try as I may I can't find enough words to adequately describe God, but I do know that by truly knowing Him, we develop a desire for and trust in Him that surpasses all others.

If we as humans would ever go beyond just head knowledge of God and develop an intimate knowledge and trust in how loving and awesome God really is, and become familiar with God's character we would discover that nothing else compares. So wholeness is by God and it is of God and it is through God, and ultimately it is for God, anything else is incomplete.

The world's ways do not compete, and we are inadequate in ourselves. This is why so many people are hurting and living in defeat, this includes many Christians. Wholeness is not possible when we keep relying on and looking to the world, and trusting in ourselves.

The following Bible verses also present the truth of wholeness and they remind us that a relationship with Christ is the foundation for true wholeness. Ephesians 3:17-20 states, "That Christ may dwell in your hearts through faith; that you being rooted and grounded in love, may be able to comprehend with all the saints what is the width and length and depth and height, to know the love of Christ which passes knowledge; that you may be filled with all the fullness of God. Now to Him who is able to do exceedingly abundantly above all that we ask or think, according to the power that works in us."

Listen to how these verses are broken down so beautifully and clearly in the MacArthur Study Bible:

"Able to comprehend." A believer cannot understand the fullness of God's love apart from a genuine, Spirit-empowered love in his own life.

"To know the love of Christ." Not the love believers have for Christ, but the love of and from Christ that He places in our hearts before we can truly and fully love Him or anyone else.

"Which passes knowledge" Knowledge of Christ's love is far beyond the capability of human reason and experience. It is only known by those who are God's children.

"Filled with all the fullness of God." To be so strong spiritually, so compelled by divine love, that one is totally dominated by the Lord with nothing left of self. Human comprehension of the fullness of God is impossible, because even the most spiritual and wise believer cannot completely grasp the full extent of God's attributes and characteristics—His power, majesty, wisdom, love, mercy, patience, kindness and everything He is and does. But believers CAN (emphasis mine) experience the greatness of God in their lives as a result of total devotion to Him. Take a minute and read over those verses again. Does it sound like anything is lacking? God has it all covered. He is the answer!

Does this mean a problem free life? Not at all! We know we will have pain, fear, trials and tribulations....because God told us so in His word. Victory and wholeness come by knowing that in our pain, fears and trials God is the answer and that He is enough!

While reading this book and, hopefully working towards the development of personal wholeness, you will frequently see how each of the components: physical, mental, financial, spiritual and social are <u>interconnected</u>. In fact in some cases, the interconnection is so strong or so dependent upon other components that the areas of wholeness are often impossible to separate.

To help identify this I have printed and underlined the word underlined frequently. This interconnection is very interesting because it demonstrates how God has all of our life issues covered when we seek Him first. "But seek first the kingdom of God and His righteousness, and all these things shall be added unto you" (Matthew 6:33). All these things are included in wholeness.

These interconnections also provide an interesting correlation to the human body and the Church, or the body of Christ. Each part is important and each part has a specific design and function, but each part relies on the other parts to serve their function. None of the components can be left out or neglected as each of them supports and at the same time depends on the other.

The Journey begins

Once we know that Jesus is the foundation for our wholeness, and we have accepted Him into our lives, the journey and our growing up has just begun. Unfortunately, many believers think that once they are saved, they have arrived. This is not true, and as Steve Brown of Key life Ministries often says, "*it is straight from the pit of hell and it smells like smoke.*" Christians have not arrived, and this way of thinking causes many Christians to miss out on the full and joyous life Jesus offers.

To begin this journey we must acknowledge that although we have asked Jesus into our hearts and have the assurance of a heavenly home for eternity, we are still in need of His guidance, love, forgiveness, correction and wisdom.

Rather than *A* journey, the development of wholeness might better be described as a series of journeys. Some can be enjoyable while others are nerve wracking and miserable. The road has deep pot holes, we run out of gas, sometimes there are detours, and maps can be misread or outdated. Some of our journeys are short, easily arrived at and relatively uneventful, others seem to never end and make us want to give up and go back where we came from.

The journey we are traveling consists solely of our choices. Yes, the choices of others, misfortune and sometimes even tragedy touches our lives, but how we respond to these things is OUR choice. Our choices are supposed to line up with the word of God, but you already knew that didn't you?

The journey never ends

The journey towards wholeness is an active and on-going process. This means we are to be working towards and taking intentional steps or actions that put what we know to use in our lives, everyday. This endeavor is not meant to be a temporary fix just for present improvements, but to become a lifestyle that we follow every day, so that we can enjoy these benefits all the days we have on this earth, and use these benefits to reach others.

Unfortunately once some people taste success or reach a mountain top, they go back to their old eating habits, stop exercising, stop saving money, neglect to spend time with God, or re-engage in unhealthy or ungodly activities. In order to continue to enjoy the benefits and peace that accompanies wholeness it is imperative for us to continue to engage in the same behaviors and make the same type of choices that got us there.

How many of us know someone who has gone on a diet, lost weight, and reached their goal? After they reached their goal they eventually return to their old eating habits and their prior activity, or no activity level. In time they gain back all the weight they lost, plus a little extra. Maybe this someone is you. It would have been much healthier to develop an eating plan that can be followed for life (a lifestyle) and benefited a person's health for life. A healthy lifestyle is what everyone needs....not a diet. Just look at the first part of that word....*die*! Not a very encouraging thought.

On this often difficult journey towards wholeness is it encouraging to know and remind ourselves that wholeness, although it takes a while, is possible and it is God's will for His children. We can know this by referring to Philippians 1:6, "Being confident of this very thing, that he who has begun a good work in you will complete it until the day of Christ Jesus."

Wholeness—A life fully trusting in, surrendered to and lived for God!

Chapter 4

SEVEN REASONS WHOLENESS IS IMPORTANT

Most of us want to be our best. We want good paying jobs, nice homes, good health, respect and recognition from others. There are infinite self-help books available to help us reach these goals. Some of these books are helpful, but some are a complete waste of time and money. The thing we must look out for is the SELF part of these books. Our efforts to be whole should be motivated by the desire to be whole so that we can be effective, compassionate, knowledgeable, equipped and resourceful workers for Christ. Just a reminder: this desire is not one that we are naturally born with in our sinful flesh. It is a desire that only God gives and develops in a willing heart.

There is nothing wrong with wanting to do and be your best. Our Heavenly Father provided us with gifts and resources so that we could effectively and successfully operate on His behalf. As Christians we know that we were bought for a price. The precious blood of Jesus was shed to pay for us to have an eternal life in Heaven. Now, we are His children, His servants, His ambassadors to a lost world. The gifts and resources He gave us are to be used to build His Kingdom. My prayers are that through this book you will come to see the importance of your personal wholeness for this calling.

Why is wholeness important?

Reason # 1. The personal wholeness of every believer or saint is important because it lends to the building up of the body of Christ, which helps prepare us for the work of ministry. Some of God's provisions to help build His children are offered through the gifts of service for the work of ministry. Some of them are listed in Ephesians 4:11-12, "And He Himself gave some to be apostles, some prophets, some evangelists, and some pastors and teachers, for the equipping of the saints for the work of ministry, for the edifying of the body of Christ."

Have you ever thought of yourself as a saint? Saints are those who God has set apart from sin to Himself, and made holy through faith in Jesus. You dear believer are a saint!

Equipping refers to restoring something to its original condition, or being made fit or complete. The equipping of Christ's ambassadors is necessary for the work of ministry to be completed. This work is the spiritual service required of every Christian, not just church leaders.

Equipping is not immediate, it takes some time, and the desired results are stated in the next verse. Ephesians 4:13 says, "till we all come to the unity of the faith and the knowledge of the Son of God, to a perfect man, to the measure of the stature of the fullness of Christ." Wow, talk about a tall expectation. The measure of the fullness of Christ. This verse clearly states that there are high standards for the body of Christ and that we are to work towards excellence, for His glory. This development doesn't just happen accidentally, it is a process. The first word [till] in the verse above indicates this.

When we are equipped and the Church is built up, we are more able to make an impact on the world for Christ. The process of developing wholeness is a journey that helps us acquire wisdom and develop strength, patience, obedience and faith, so that we can become more prepared to reach others for God.

Interconnection—God has a plan and a purpose for all of His children. When we believers operate according to his plan we help each other, when we help each other we ourselves are helped and the body of Christ is edified.

—Helping others is what God requires of us for the good of community. Jesus' life demonstrated this perfectly. Everything He did was out of love for His creation. Our obedience to this requirement is a manifestation of our love for God.

—We all want a purpose and passion in our life. It is very reinforcing and enjoyable to use the gifts that God has given us to pursue this purpose.

God knows this and very early on He gave man a purpose. In Genesis 2:15 we are told, "Then the Lord God took the man and put him in the garden of Eden to tend and keep it." Some translations say to cultivate and guard. Regardless of the translation, we see here that God gave Adam a job, a purpose and God did this *before* the fall of man. Work is not intended as a curse. When we work, produce, create, nurture and protect we are imitating our Father.

—When each of us is operating in and using the gifts He has given us, on His behalf, we are operating in unity and are more effective as a body. To make this a little more practical, think about walking. If one foot is stepping to the back and one foot is stepping forward, no progress will be made. When the body of Christ is moving towards two different agendas, progress is difficult. The agenda of the body of Christ should be fulfilling the Great Commission. Opportunities to fulfill this agenda are numerous and diverse.

Sometimes the using of these gifts and the work of ministry is difficult and draining. So in order to equip the saints by using these gifts we all need spiritual strength, which is the foundation for wholeness. Physical, mental, social and financial wellness can also help us with this equipping of the saints.

Reason # 2. Wholeness is important in the life of a believer because God wants it for us. He desires for His children to experience this blessing. Look at John 10:10, "The thief does not come except to steal, and to kill, and to destroy. I have come that they may have life, and that they may have it more abundantly." God loves His children and He wants us to experience all the good he has planned for us.

Our wholeness is a gift from our loving and generous Father. He promises us a life far better than we could ever envision. This desire of God is further confirmed to us in I Corinthians 2:9, "But as it is written: eye has not seen, nor ear heard, nor have entered into the heart of man the things which God has prepared for those who love Him." What a beautiful, comforting and exciting verse. It is basically saying that we humans can't possibly imagine the things God has planned for those who love Him. This is just one of many promises God makes, and remember God keeps His promises.

We must remind ourselves that wholeness is a gift from God and only from Him. Our Savior is the only one who can meet all our needs. No person, money, status, hobby, body weight, title or degree can provide this. Our problems come when we look to people or things to fulfill us rather than seeking our True Provider. "For my people have committed two evils; They have forsaken Me, the fountain of living waters, And hewn themselves cisterns—broken cisterns that can hold no water" (Jeremiah 2:13).

Since we are realizing wholeness as a gift from God, consider this verse in James 1:17, "Every good gift and every perfect gift is from above, and comes down from the Father of lights, with whom there is no variation or shadow of turning." Only God can give perfect gifts. When blessings come into our lives we must make it a regular practice to stop and intentionally thank God. This, by the way, helps with our spiritual wellness.

Consider one more verse that tells us that God likes to give His children gifts.

"If you then, being evil, know how to give good gifts to your children, how much more will your heavenly Father give the Holy Spirit to those who ask Him!" (Luke 11:13). Most of us enjoy giving gifts to those we love and care for, and it pleases us when on occasion we get it right and the recipient of our gift actually enjoys and appreciates what we give them. If we human beings, who are limited and flawed can give good gifts, how much more can our Father give? And His gifts are perfect.

"Let them shout for joy and be glad, who favor my righteous cause and let them say continually, Let the Lord be magnified, Who has pleasure in the prosperity of His servants"(Psalm 35:27). God loves giving good gifts to His children because He delights in the prosperity of His children. He loves it most of all when we know the gifts were from and especially designed for us by Him. I love how John Piper put it:

"God is most glorified when we are most satisfied in Him."

Reason # 3. Wholeness is important in the life of a believer because it keeps us humble, and aware of our need for God. The development of wholeness is a growing process that at times is very difficult and frustrating. We will fail, get angry, get discouraged, get disappointed, and experience pain or maybe betrayal. These struggles teach us to seek, lean on and obey God. Without difficult times we would never have the opportunity to live in the truth that God is our source…regardless of the specific type of need or struggle we have, God is our source. These times of trials are a beneficial and necessary part of God's training program for His servants. James 1:2-4 states, "My brethren, count it all joy when you fall into various trials, knowing that the testing of your faith produces patience. But let patience have its perfect work, that you may be perfect and complete lacking nothing."

Not only do these trials keep us humble, they also prepare, educate and shape us so that we may help others facing the same trials.

Interconnection. The social implications of helping others with their struggles are easily seen. Our spiritual wellness is demonstrated when we imitate Christ in the helping and comforting of others. "Blessed be the God and Father of our Lord Jesus Christ, the father of mercies and God of all comfort, who comforts us in all our tribulation, that we may be able to comfort those who are in any trouble, with the comfort with which we ourselves are comforted by God"(2 Corinthians 1:3-4).

What great verses of reassurance. It says that He is the Father of mercies and God of all comfort. Notice that it says God of all comfort, in all tribulation, in any trouble. I think after reading this verse, we can have peace knowing that there is nothing in our lives that God can't handle.

Comfort is just one of many blessings God provides for His children, and as children of God we are to be conduits through which His favor and love flow. This favor and love are intended to help prevent the misfortune, pain and suffering of others. I think that each of us has been comforted, encouraged or inspired by someone who overcame struggles and adversities. It helps people in the midst of a crisis to see and know that others have found recovery and victory over similar painful and overwhelming trials.

Reason # 4. The journey leading to wholeness in our lives teaches us obedience to God. There are obvious benefits in the development of wholeness, but ultimately the benefits are in the process not just the desired outcome of wholeness. This principle behind the benefits of process brings to mind the stories printed about the numerous lottery winners or those who came into a large amount of money very easily, and then file bankruptcy. Its better stated as *found* money rather than *earned* money. People tend to spend money differently when it was easily obtained or found, rather than when they put time, effort and discipline into earning it. These winners came upon the money without knowing how to develop it so they did not know how to maintain it. Our wholeness is like that. Once we develop, live in and enjoy it we have to know how to continue to maintain it and that comes through the process of developing it.

As followers of Christ this process of working towards wholeness is accomplished through our obedience to God. This is not an easy task, it requires a daily dying to the flesh and it often requires struggling or suffering, in fact we are informed of this in Romans 5:3-5, "And not only that, but we also glory in tribulation, knowing that tribulation produces perseverance; and perseverance, character; and character, hope. Now hope does not disappoint, because the love of God has been poured out in our hearts by the Holy Spirit who was given to us." It is odd but it seems that problems and pain are often necessary for God to get our attention, and it is often through these difficult times that we learn and grow.

For just a moment think about Christ, and look at Hebrews 5:8, "Though He was a Son, yet He learned obedience by the things which He suffered." If Jesus learned obedience, perhaps we all have some learning to do. But, Jesus didn't need to suffer or learn obedience because of any mistakes or disobedience.

He was perfect and understood obedience perfectly. Jesus humbled Himself to learn. He learned obedience for the same reason that He paid for our sins on the cross, to confirm that He was fully human and He experienced suffering to the fullest. Christ's obedience was also necessary to fulfill the will of God and willingly offer Himself as the perfect sacrifice, taking on all the sins of the world. Commentary: John Macarthur, Study Bible.

Jesus performed in completion the greatest and most painful act to ever take place in all of history. It is unnecessary for me to say this was not easy. I will merely say that what Jesus did for us on the cross epitomized the term "dying to the flesh." Nothing we are asked to endure will compare to this act of love.

The key factor to obedience is learning to submit to God and not our flesh. Unfortunately because we have spent so much of our lives obeying the flesh and pursuing its desires, it is a very difficult habit to break. Maintaining physical comfort is a lifestyle for all of us. We were born into it and we have lived it so long it becomes natural and very easy for us to follow. We will continue on in this behavior unless we seek, submit to, trust and obey our Heavenly Father. Isn't it easier to obey someone you trust?

This process of learning obedience by suffering is not fun, and often times it doesn't seem to mesh with wellness. Suffering however is frequently necessary in the development of our obedience. Regardless of the sufferings we are called to endure, and regardless of the uncertainty, pain and seeming injustice, we do know because the Bible says.... and we must remind ourselves, that this will be used for good. "And we know that all things work together for good to those who love God, to those who are called according to His purpose" (Romans 8:28). I have probably relied on this verse more times than any other.

Reason # 5. Wholeness in the lives of God's children glorifies the Father. If you are a parent, you can relate to this because you delight in the success, health, happiness, accomplishments, wisdom and wise choices of your children, it is a reflection on you and it brings you great joy. This is clearly what we are being told in Matthew 5:16, "Let your light shine before men, that they may see your good works and glorify your Father who is in Heaven." God displays His power for all to see through His creation. Mankind and his good works are God's creation.

Many people in our world are confused, angry, scared and hurting. They want an answer; they want hope, acceptance and security. Unfortunately many are seeking for these things in the wrong places and teachings. Satan is doing all he can to promote these wrong places and wrong teachings. He is the father of lies. He earned this title because he is good and very effective at deceiving people. "Whose minds the god of this age has blinded, who do not believe, lest the light of the gospel of the glory of Christ, who is the image of God, should shine on them"(2 Corinthians 4:4).

When God's children demonstrate wholeness it sets His children apart. When the watching world sees us demonstrate honesty, purity and integrity in our choices and words, and when they see God's children treat others with love, respect, compassion, empathy and generosity it shows the world there is a difference. That difference is God. It is most definitely not because we are good, but because God is good. "For I know that in me (that is, in my flesh) nothing good dwells; for to will is present with me, but how to perform what is good I do not find" (Rom. 7:18). Even when we know what is right, and we want to do or say the right things, we often still do or say the wrong things. Our daily actions, the word we speak and the choices we make can be a testimony to those watching. In our daily strivings and choices, we are here to give Him glory in all things.

Reason # 6. Wellness in the body of Christ helps us fulfill the Great Commission. Found in Matthew 28:19-20 it reads, "Go therefore and make disciples of all the nations, baptizing them in the name of the Father, and of the Son and of the Holy Spirit, teaching them to observe all things that I have commanded you; and lo, I am with you always, even to the end of the age."

Look at the first word of the Great Commission, Go. How do we go if we are broke, weak, angry, hungry, apathetic, depressed and spiritually bankrupt ourselves? The body of Christ needs wholeness. So not only is it a beautiful gift from God it is also a very necessary and functional tool from God.

Wholeness is an equipping possible only through God. We may experience physical wellness and financial wealth, but at what expense? Numerous individuals have a variety of social activities and outstanding academic achievements, but without a spiritual foundation built by, with and on God, these are merely nice things that can help us experience comfort and the praise of men, but they are temporary and can be lost. Typically when we see someone in the world who has excelled and achieved at higher levels than the majority of others, we will see that other areas of their lives are lacking because these areas have been neglected to pursue an idol. What is an idol?

"It is anything more important to you than God, anything that absorbs your heart and imagination more than God, anything you seek to give you what only God can give. An idol is whatever you look at and say, in your

heart of hearts, "If I have that, then I'll feel my life has meaning, then I'll know I have value, then I'll feel significant and secure." Taken from Tim Keller's, *Counterfeit Gods.*

When we as Christians seek, go after and allow these idols in our lives we are interfering with God's provision and we not only hurt ourselves, we hurt the work of the Kingdom. These idols cannot provide forgiveness or wholeness.

In all of our strivings we are told "Whatever you do, do it heartily, as to the Lord and not to men." (Colossians 3:23). Fulfilling the Great Commission is what followers of Christ are to do. So when that verse says: *"whatever you do"* it includes this command. Doing things heartily requires hard work, time, consistency, commitment and often sacrifice. The development of wholeness supports us in this striving.

Reason # 7. Developing Wholeness is being a good steward. Look at the definition of a steward—a person who manages the property or financial affairs of another, a person who has charge of the household of another. As Christians we have been entrusted with various resources, blessings and responsibilities, all of which belong to God. When wholeness is lived out in our lives, our financial, physical, spiritual, social, mental and emotional wellbeing are attended to, strengthened and used to impact the world for Christ.

To be an effective and faithful steward, we need: Godly wisdom, adequate knowledge to make sound decisions, compassion and concern for others and the physical or financial resources necessary to maintain and nurture that which has been placed in our care. Being a good steward includes using our God given blessing to bless others. We are to allow the gifts of God to flow to those around us. We are to give as God has given to us.

Stop for just a minute and think of all the things God has given or provided for you. Start with the simple physical things you see around you, then think about the unseen spiritual benefits He offers, what about eternal life and a Friend who is ever present, all loving and all powerful. We add to this mercy and forgiveness, comfort, hope, peace, strength and wisdom. We as finite human beings are not aware of all an infinite God has done or can do. We can't fully understand His goodness. If, however each of us would be conduits of the good things we do know of, tremendous numbers of people could be reached.

The world is so deceived and confused about the message of the gospel. Francis Chan put it better in his video "Stop and think." *"The whole message of the Bible is not about this God who wants to take from you; it is about this God who wants to give to you."* God frequently gives through His children. He uses us imperfect physical human beings to bless and minister to other physical human beings.

These blessings we are to share are not always financial or material things, both of which are important and necessary to live in this world, but they are temporal and can be lost or destroyed in an instant. This is not to say we can ignore financial or material needs. We have to be sensitive to personal needs and meet people where they are, just as Jesus did.

Once we have listened to a person in need and addressed their physical tangible needs we then need to tell them of God's blessings which are eternal and incorruptible. When we introduce someone to God we have introduced them to the most powerful and complete life changing source available. Consider your personal resources right now, not just financial, but your time, training, clothing, your home, extra produce from your garden, special skills and personal experience with difficult life events. All of these can be used and present you with an opportunity to share your blessings. Consider some of the following examples that are probably present needs in your area right now.

—Bless an elderly or disabled person by mowing their lawn, raking their leaves, taking their trash to the curb on trash day or helping them move something heavy.

—Lonely people can be blessed when someone takes the time to visit with them or just stops and takes an interest in them, or invites them to church.

—People dealing with fear and rejection can be ministered to when we offer: time, encouragement, comfort or wisdom to them.

—Children raised in a fatherless home would love a man to play catch with them.

—Tell an un-churched person about how much Jesus loves them.

—Read to someone who can't read for themselves.

—Stand up and defend those who are weak or who are afraid to stand.

—Help a widow with home or auto repairs.

—Mentor a high school drop out who has decided to go back to school.

—Baby-sit for a single mom or dad who has no family around to help them.

—Single parents struggling with bills or feeding their children are blessed when we feed them or purchase groceries for them out of the abundance that God has provided for us.

—Buy and have lunch with a homeless person or a lonely person who feels forgotten.

The list could go on and on. Above are just a few ways that we can minister to and bless the people around us.

According to the word of God we can know that wholeness is a part of God's plan for His children. We also know that God loved the world so much that He sent His son to die for the world's sins. These two truths being known, one more <u>Interconnection</u> can be made. God blesses us and helps us develop wholeness so that we can be a blessing to others by meeting them where their level of need is.

This theme has been stated previously, but it is the foundation for this entire book so it needs to be repeated. Our personal wholeness is of God, by God, through God, with God and to be used for God.

Chapter 5

THE EIGHTH REASON WHOLENESS IS IMPORTANT

It helps develop unity in the body of Christ

I gave this eighth reason a chapter to itself due to the fact that an entire book or actually several books could be written about this topic. I also believe that it is very important, and I didn't want it to be read over quickly or dismissed because it was listed as the last reason that wholeness is important.

When speaking physically we know what the whole body means. The whole physical body includes every visible and non-visible body part, from the top of our heads to the bottom of our feet and every organ, bone, muscle, fluid, ligament and tendon in-between. Each of these body parts was designed for a specific function and each part is designed to be helpful to the entire body.

The whole body I am referring to in this chapter is not the physical body that is made of flesh and blood. The body I am referring to is the body of Christ as mentioned in Ephesians 1:22-23, "And He put all things under His feet, and gave Him to be head over all things to the church, which is His body, the fullness of Him who fills all in all." Verse 23 clearly states that the church is His body.

We need to remember that this body has many members with many functions, just as the human body does. We are told this in Romans 12:4-5, "For as we have many members in one body, but all the members do not have the same function, so we, being many, are one body in Christ, and individually members of one another." So we clearly see that the body of Christ has many members, and each member has a different function, much like our physical bodies. It is so neat how the Bible frequently makes spiritual analogies through the use of physical and tangible terms. God knew He had to break it down to our level. He teaches us by using examples that we actually see, feel and put to use in our every day lives.

God desires unity in His body. He loves the church and it breaks His heart when we are opposing and hurting each other. Lets go to John 17: 9, 11b, 21-24 to look at the: who, what, why, when and where of this desire.

Who? "I pray for them. I do not pray for the world but for those whom You have given Me, for they are Yours." In verse 9, Jesus prays specifically for His followers.

What was He praying for? Read on to the last part of John 17:11, "Holy Father keep through Your name those whom you have given Me, that they may be one as We are." Jesus wants His church to be one, as He and the Father are one.

Why? Verses 21-23 tell us. "That they all may be one, as You, Father, are in Me, and I in You; that they also may be one in Us, that the world may believe that You sent Me. And the glory You gave Me I have given them, that they may be one just as We are one: I in them, and You in Me; that they may be made perfect in one, and that the world may know that You have sent Me, and have loved them as You have loved Me."

Two reasons for why are listed as: 1. So the church may be made perfect in one. 2. So through this unity, which God wants in His church, the world may believe and know that God sent Jesus. Unfortunately the unbelieving world frequently sees division, competition, bitterness and contentions in many of our churches today. Our divisions get in the way of the love of Jesus.

Where & When ? Both are answered in verse 24 "Father, I desire that they also whom You gave Me may be with Me where I am, that they may behold My glory which You have given Me; for you loved Me before the foundation of the world." Wow, have you ever thought of that? Jesus wants us where He is. He really, really loves us. And since we know that Jesus is an infinite being who always was and always will be, we know that our being with Him will be for eternity.

To put it briefly and succinctly, God wants His church to be one, so that the world will know about Him, and so that His children are made perfect in Him, will glorify Him, and can live with Him forever in heaven. Knowing this is Jesus' desire, we also know that any thing Jesus loves and desires, Satan hates, opposes and seeks to destroy.

Satan opposes the church in many ways; one of those is through division, which is a very effective and destructive tool. In fact division of the kingdom of God is why we humans live in a fallen world. Satan didn't want to worship God, Satan wanted to be worshiped. He gathered together with some of the angels and convinced them that his way was better than Gods. The angels were deceived and chose to follow Satan rather than God. Through deception, Satan convinced Adam and Eve that God was holding out on them. Their misbelief led them to commit man's original sin. This sin divided man from the perfect creation of God, a creation that met all of man's needs. More sadly though, it created division between man and God, and destroyed the perfect fellowship that God originally designed. Satan lives and operates to destroy man, the image of God.

Division is also used by Satan as a tool to prevent the fellowship of Christian brothers and sisters, and ultimately to prevent the reconciliation of creation with its Creator. We are told that division has no place in the body of Christ. I Corinthians 12:25, "That there should be no schism in the body, but that the members should have the same care for one another." If the body of Christ is divided and wasting time, energy, passion and resources on their petty differences and practices, they are reducing the time, energy, passion and resources that should be used to build each other up, so that each one is better equipped to do their part in building God's Kingdom.

By focusing on and disputing about temporal and non-essential issues, the church is not adhering to the affirmation given to every believer found in Philippians 3:12-14, "Not that I have already attained, or am already perfected; but I press on, that I may lay hold of that for which Christ Jesus has also laid hold of me. Brethren, I do not count myself to have apprehended; but one thing I do, forgetting those things which are behind and reaching forward to those things which are ahead. I press toward the goal for the prize of the upward call of God in Christ Jesus."

The goal is the upward call of God, which is broken down into one thing, the pursuing of Christ-likeness while we are on this earth. This is what every believer should strive for and focus upon. The prize is ultimately becoming like Christ. The completion of becoming Christ-like can only happen in heaven, however if we make this our genuine endeavor, much improvement and maturity will take place while we are here. When each member of the body of Christ is honestly devoted, and deliberately follows and obeys their Father, each can become more like Christ. When operating like Christ we take our eyes off of our own personal and selfish agendas and promote His. Being Christ-like is wholeness. Nothing is missing, nothing is broken and nothing is lacking.

Another obstacle to unity in the body of Christ is limited human perceptions. The problem is that our own perceptions are typically narrow and frequently formed out of self-serving motives. This leads to misguided attempts to promote God's agenda based solely on our own understanding, and it can become a source of conflict and division.

This is common between the numerous denominations. It is effective because it is very deceitful. It appears that we are fighting a Holy battle with righteous intentions. All of us are under the belief that, our denomination really gets it right. We will all however, sometimes concede that there are a few others from different denominations that will be in Heaven. But we have all chosen a denomination that most conforms to our belief system or a set of values that we have been raised up in, or that we might even be following out of habit and comfort rather than personal conviction and Biblical truths. Considering the various denominations there are today, we need to remember that denominations were not a creation of God. "Now I plead with you, brethren, by the name of our Lord Jesus Christ, that you all speak the same thing, and that there be no divisions among you, but that you be perfectly joined together in the same mind and in the same judgment" (I Corinthians 1:10).

What is the same thing we are to speak? How are we to be joined in the same mind and same judgment? 2 John: 9 states; "Whoever transgresses and does not abide in the doctrine of Christ does not have God. He who abides in the doctrine of Christ has both the Father and Son." We are to abide in the doctrine of Christ. The doctrine of Christ is based on faith in God and His entire word, not just one verse. Frequently we human beings find a verse and fail to read the verses proceeding and following that verse or neglect to consider the circumstances during which the verse was written. This can lead to the development of a very narrow and often incorrect understanding of that verse.

These incorrect understandings are so powerful and convincing that people throughout history have used them as the basis for the creation of numerous denominations and even to fuel wars. It is imperative for each of us to personally commit to reading the Bible consistently, and develop a personal understanding that God will give. It might be a little uncomfortable or even frightening because, God may reveal a truth to us in His word that is contrary to a belief we have built our lives around.

If each of us builds our lives on our personal shaping of the scriptures to fulfill our personal agenda that fits within our personal level of comfort, we then miss out on the life changing truths it offers. This can also lead us to forget the fact that the scripture is written for the benefit of all mankind. His word is full of infinite wisdom. It is powerful and living. We are all to live according to all Biblical principles, not just one verse.

If each and every believer and child of God were putting authentic efforts into the development of being Christ-like, and if we would diligently seek to know God by spending time in His word and obeying Him, our attempts to work and live in unity could be more productive. God loves His entire family. He has enough love and resources to meet all of our needs. He wants us to love each other, enjoy fellowship with each other and work together to glorify Him and build His kingdom. Unity based upon the doctrine of Christ is good for the entire body of Christ because it gives us strength, encouragement and united resources to use for the work of God.

The world was against and eventually crucified Jesus because He spoke the truth. His followers will be rejected and hated by the world, the Bible tells us this, in fact we are told not to think it strange when the world hates us because it first hated Jesus. We would be wise to heed this truth offered by Jesus. We know the world is looking to oppress, devalue, persecute and in some countries even execute Christians. The word execution may sound drastic, but it is a reality and according to Center for Study of Global Christianity, a Christian is killed for their faith every five minutes in the world.

The bitterness, hatred and oppression faced from the world can be frightening and discouraging. It should prompt us to unite and work towards learning to love, encourage and care for each other. The world is working to destroy Christian values and beliefs and they are aiming at followers of Christ to accomplish this. If the world is against us, we should not be against each other. "If a kingdom is divided against itself, that kingdom cannot stand. And if a house is divided against itself, that house cannot stand" (Mark 3:24-25).

All of those who love Jesus and know that He is the savior of the world, have asked Him to be their personal savior and want His kingdom to come are part of the family of God. It is a big family and it would help us all if we could set aside little insignificant differences that will not matter in eternity and focus on issues of eternal value. If we serve and love the same God we should learn to serve and love each other.

Chapter 6

EXPECTATIONS FOR CHRISTIANS

There are many titles that people use for a person once they have accepted Jesus into their lives. We often hear or use the terms: believers, followers, Christians, children of God, servants, ambassadors, stewards, brothers and sisters in Christ. There are also some that aren't so nice. Regardless of the title you use, I want us to think of ourselves as God's army. Does that bring to your mind the song you used to sing in children's church? "I'm in the lord's army." If so, stop reading and go ahead and sing it through.

The commander in Chief is the Lord, He is the Ultimate Ruler! He is above all powers and principalities! Knowing this, it is imperative for us to be equipped and ready for the battles and obstacles that life will throw at us. Now, is the song: "Onward Christian soldiers" coming to mind?

God has a high calling for His army and being a solider isn't for wimps, in fact a life that is Christ-like can be very challenging and difficult. It is difficult for a couple of reasons, first, because Satan endlessly works to stop the spreading of the truth of God. He knows that when people hear and then believe in the truth of God, lives can be changed. Satan is very aware of God's power; this is why he works in such a vicious, aggressive, deceitful and continual manner. He knows his time is limited, that God is the ultimate ruler and one day every knee will bow to God. In the meantime Satan doesn't want any more humans accepting Jesus into their lives. Satan doesn't want the kingdom of God to grow.

Another reason for our difficulties is because we as humans typically operate according to our own personal desires and limited wisdom. Fortunately for us, God is able and willing to meet us in our weakness and provide the strength and direction we need for this calling. When we get tired and want to quit or when we feel inadequate and overwhelmed, we need to refer to 2 Timothy 3:16-17, "All scripture is given by inspiration of God, and is profitable for doctrine, for reproof, for correction, for instruction in righteousness, that the man of God may be complete, thoroughly equipped for every good work". God can complete and equip us for every good work, and He provided the Bible through His divine inspiration for this purpose. He gave it to guide, strengthen, comfort, encourage and inform us.

The Bible is to be His children's handbook for life. It was written for our benefit, and in it exist all the answers to a life of wholeness. It is most effective when we refer to and follow it in all matters. Read, apply and repeat!

Take a look now at some of the commands and expectations that God has for His children. As you read, stop and think about how difficult some of these expectations are in real life. Our personal wholeness helps equip us for all of these expectations.

<u>Love God and Love People</u>: "Jesus said to him, you shall love the Lord your God with all your heart, with all your soul, and with all your mind. This is the first and great commandment. And the second is like it: you shall love your neighbor as yourself. On these two commandments hang all the Law and the Prophets" (Matthew 22:37-40). Jesus did not say its o.k. to love God just a little, He told us to love him with all of our being. He also tells us to love our neighbor as we love ourselves.

These commandments are so important that all the other Laws hang on them. All of us should know that love is more than an emotion or a feeling, which can change with circumstances. Love is alive, it is being and doing. It is showing, telling, listening, helping, building and giving. The song by D.C. Talk titled, "Luv is a verb" sums it up nicely. The entire being and life of Christ on earth was the perfect example of love, everything He did was for the good of others. This is difficult for us because we as human beings are born sinners with a very selfish disposition. The acceptance of Jesus and His love into our lives can help with this.

To be like Christ: Ephesians 5:1-2 tells us, "Therefore be imitators of God as dear children. And walk in love, as Christ also has loved us and given Himself for us, an offering and a sacrifice to God for a sweet-smelling aroma."

Jesus' life exemplifies wholeness because Jesus lived a perfect, sinless life completely submitted to and unified with God. This commission given to us is difficult. How can we fallen, sinful and selfish children be like the Holy God of the universe? By imitating Jesus, Who came to earth not only to be our savior, but also to provide an example for us to follow. Left unto ourselves we can't be like Him, this is possible only through Him. Jesus has paid the price, and has ultimately secured victory for His believers. We learn how to walk in this victory though full trust and obedience to Him.

Be Holy: In 1 Peter 1:15 we are told, "But as He who called you is holy, you also be holy in all your conduct". That is a pretty tall order. Holy means being separated from evil or set apart. It can also mean sacred, not ordinary.

Our world needs this today, but in order for us to be holy, it might mean that we have to give up or change some things in our lives. This being holy means, not trying to blend in with the world or becoming consumed with trying to please people in order to gain their approval and acceptance. It means we live our lives and make our choices in obedience to God.

Being holy is very challenging because people can be rude, demanding, difficult, deceitful and just plain mean. Circumstances can be unfair, painful and shocking. To be holy requires spiritual wellness, which requires first of all a personal relationship with Jesus. To grow and develop this relationship we must specifically set aside time with Him and in His word on a daily basis, and then we follow through by applying and living in His truths. Holiness is possible only through Him. Jesus was holy and this affected the entire world.

It takes humbleness, patience, wisdom, love, obedience to God and self-sacrifice to be holy. Philippians 2:3 admonishes, "Let nothing be done through selfish ambition or conceit, but in lowliness of mind let each esteem others better than himself." I truly believe that our world would change if every believer made this verse a functional part of their everyday life. It is what Jesus did when He willingly died on the cross, and it is the most powerful event to ever take place in history.

Interconnection—Spiritual, Mental & Social

To be the salt and light: Matthew 5:13-14, 16 relates, "You are the salt of the earth; but if salt loses its flavor, how shall it be seasoned? It is then good for nothing but to be thrown out and trampled under foot by men, You are the light of the world. A city that is set on a hill cannot be hidden. Let your light so shine before men, that they may see your good works and glorify your Father in heaven."

Unfortunately our world is a dark place, and this is partially because the church has not been the salt and light. We look around and too often see many Christians who are depressed, angry, fearful, filing bankruptcy, getting divorced, cursing people out, stealing from their employers, committing adultery, dealing with addictions, suffering from lifestyle diseases, and handling life's struggles the same way the lost world is. To be salt and light we must be spiritually well as all other components of wholeness flow from this.

Interconnection—Our spiritual wellness manifests itself in all we do. It can help the world see Jesus.

To be Christ's ambassadors: II Corinthians 5:20 says, "Therefore, we are ambassadors for Christ, as though God were pleading through us: we implore you on Christ's behalf, be reconciled to God." Stop and think of the magnitude of that verse and calling.

God is pleading through us…. What a high calling. The U.S. sends ambassadors all over the world. These ambassadors learn the culture, norms, languages and values of the nations where they are going. This takes time, effort, work and hours of studying. As Christ's ambassadors, we must ask ourselves if each of us put the time, effort and dedication into this calling.

Interconnection—All areas of our wholeness help us serve in this position.

Be world preachers and teachers: In Mark 16:15 we are told, "Go into the all the world and preach the gospel to every creature." If we are to go into all the world, financial resources are needed. In order to teach and preach we must know the gospel. Traveling can be demanding and mission trips often require physical labor, it will be much easier for us if we are in good physical health. Effective communication skills and compassion will also be very useful in helping us connect with people.

Interconnection—Mental, Social, Financial, Spiritual and Physical)

Be a good walker, generous & forgiving: Matthew 5:39–42 commands us, "But whoever slaps you on your right cheek, turn the other to him also, If anyone wants to sue you and take your tunic, let him also have your cloak, And whoever compels you to go one mile, go two with him. Give him who asks you, and from him who wants to borrow from you do not turn away." These verses encourage us to do more than we are asked.

Interconnection—Financial, Emotional, Spiritual, Physical and Social. Are you wondering where emotional wellness comes in? I think it takes a pretty emotionally strong person to let someone slap you twice. I certainly am not there yet. Another thought, financial wellness would be nice here too, because, if I give my tunic and cloak away, I would need to go buy a new one for myself....well, I wouldn't need to, but I'd sure like to.

<u>Be strong:</u> Romans 15:1 states, "We then who are strong ought to bear the scruples of the weak, and not to please ourselves." Notice this didn't say *if* you are strong. It says: *we then who are strong.* It is spoken as a fact and as an imperative to believers. It is an expectation we should take to heart and put into practice. When we are struggling and ready to give up due to our own personal problems it is difficult to be strong for others. This is just one of the many reasons our wholeness is so important.

<u>Interconnection</u>—This Verse can be referring to Mental, Emotional, Spiritual or Physical strength. When Christians are spiritually strong they are better equipped to deal with any struggles.

<u>Be Peaceful:</u> Romans 12:18 says, "If it is possible, as much as depends on you, live peaceably with all men." In life ultimately the only thing we truly have control over is ourselves, and at times controlling ourselves seems almost impossible. We frequently attempt to manipulate, guilt or scare others into doing what we want them to do. We can blame them for making us mad or we can choose to get even so they don't take advantage of us or lie to us again. We can settle the score and really get even. Or, we can do our part and live in a peaceable manner. It takes two to argue and disagree however, it requires only one to take a Christ-like step and exercise self-control and obedience to God. This step will help in dealing with obstinate or angry people. Imagine what would happen if all of society did what they could to live peaceably.

<u>Interconnection</u>—Spiritual, Mental/Emotional & Social

<u>Walk in love:</u> Ephesians 5:2 relates, "as Christ also has loved us and given Himself for us, an offering and a sacrifice to God." What is love? It is a demonstration of the fruits of the spirit found in Galatians 5:22-23. "But the fruit of the Spirit is love, joy, peace, longsuffering, kindness, goodness and faithfulness, gentleness, self-control. Against

such there is no law." Did you catch that? It is like Paul is saying "Hey there is no law against being nice and kind to others"

Interconnection—Social, Spiritual and Physical. Physical is listed here because love is demonstrated through what we do not just what we say. Longsuffering on our part may require that we be physically uncomfortable or perform some difficult physical tasks.

Be Jiminy Cricket to someone; Galatians 6:1&2, "Brethren, if a man is overtaken in any trespass, you who are spiritual restore such a one in a spirit of gentleness, considering yourself lest you also be tempted. Bear one another's burdens, and so fulfill the law of Christ."

We all need a word of warning from time to time. The Bible is always available to us, but sometimes a warning from someone we can see and audibly hear is very helpful.

When attempting to restore someone who is overtaken by any trespass, it is of utmost importance to do so in gentleness as this verse says. Mostly because that is what Jesus would do. He is the savior of the world and all power is in him, yet He is the ultimate example of love, gentleness and mercy. I think this is also a bit of a warning for the times when we get a bit too impressed with ourselves. It helps remind us that we too can be tempted and may catch ourselves in the same trespass.

That warning part of the verse could also cause us to stop and think before we say to or about someone, "Oh, they shouldn't feel that way, or they shouldn't be mad" Or "you have no reason to feel that way, you should be grateful", on what basis are we making these statements? Who are we to say how someone should feel. If we were to experience the death of a dear friend, or worse yet a child, we might get angry. If a job we've dreamed about doesn't pan out for us we might experience doubt. Maybe we've never dealt with what they are dealing with. We would be wise to be gentle when someone expresses an emotion, a weakness or a desire to us. An event could occur that would cause us to feel the same emotion or have the same desire.

The verses found in Galatians 6:1&2, makes me want to say, God is so cool! His word and His intentions are always for a Win-Win outcome. His words in that verse are meant for us to use to help others, and those words are also to help ourselves.

Interconnection—Any component of our lives can be involved in trespasses.

Grow up; Ephesians 4:14-15 tells us, "that we should no longer be children tossed to and fro and carried about with every wind of doctrine, by the trickery of men, in the cunning craftiness by which they lie in wait to deceive, but, speaking the truth in love, may grow up in all things into Him who is the head—Christ." The process of growing up is challenging enough, and it definitely requires some suffering, some experience, some pain, sacrifice and failure. We as Christians are to grow in Him. This requires that we be grounded in the knowledge of Christ through His word. Without this we too can be deceived by the trickery of men.

Do your part; Ephesians 4:16 says, "From whom the whole body joined and knit together by what every joint supplies, according to the effective working by which every part does its share, causes growth of the body for the edifying of itself in love." God made the human body in a marvelous way. Each part is so intricate and precise, and serves a specific and very necessary function. The body of Christ is like this and when every part does its share, it causes growth in the body. God has a purpose and call for each of His children. Every calling and member in this body matters and is immensely valuable.

Interconnection—I don't even have to point it out here

Glorify Him; Corinthians 6:20 reveals, "You were bought for a price: therefore glorify God in your body and in your spirit which are God's." There is nothing more powerful and valuable than the precious blood of Jesus. His blood has the power to heal, restore and cleanse us.

What is so amazing is that when we ask Jesus into our hearts to save us, He does so and covers us with *His* righteousness. When God looks and sees us, He sees the righteousness of His son. There is an old saying that goes *"He died for us, the least we can do is live for Him."* We glorify God in our bodies, when we take care of them and use them to do God's work.

Interconnection—All components of wholeness are useful here because we have the opportunity to glorify God in everything we say and everything we do.

<u>Walk in good work</u>: The more I read the Bible the more I really believe that God likes walking. The word walk or one of its forms is used 408 times in the Bible. Do you think that since it is mentioned so many times in God's word that maybe we should do a little more of it? Ephesians 2:10 reminds us, "For we are His workmanship created in Christ Jesus for good works, which God prepared beforehand that we should <u>walk</u> in them." Stop the talking and start the walking! Good works, this is what we were created for.

<u>Be Merciful</u>: Colossians 3:12 tells us, "Therefore as the elect of God, holy and beloved, put on tender mercies, kindness, humbleness of mind, meekness, longsuffering." Here again is another one of God's expectations that can only be met by having strong Spiritual, mental and emotional health. Notice the last word, *longsuffering*. Who among us really likes to suffer? We as humans do all we can to be comfortable, so we must know that this isn't a request. He doesn't say, if it is comfortable and convenient for you. He tells us to *put on* these characteristics. There is physicality in this verse "put on". The "putting on", will transpire into physical actions, but they develop and manifest themselves from our spiritual maturity.

Interconnection—spiritual, mental/emotional, physical and social

<u>Think about the good of others</u>: "Let each of us please his neighbor for his good leading to edification" (Romans 15:2). This is a pretty tough challenge and difficult command. It defies the human nature that we are all born with.We as humans typically operate out of self-

serving motives. This pleasing our neighbor for *their* good can even be a bit painful at times.

We just reviewed a few of the many expectations Christ has of believers, and quite honestly sometimes it seems that doing the right thing is very difficult and almost impossible. But Jesus tells us differently in Matthew 11:29-30, "Take my yoke upon you and learn from Me, for I am gentle and lowly in heart and you will find rest for your souls. For my yoke is easy and My burden is light."

If the yoke of Jesus is easy, why do we fail so often and get so tired and discouraged? The difficulty comes when we look to ourselves and others to be our help and strength. God never intended for us to do it on our own. We can also make things more difficult by focusing on the challenge at hand rather than trusting in the sufficiency of God.

Jesus' yoke is easy; we are to be telling the lost world the greatest news to ever exist. Who wouldn't want to know this? We have a very real enemy who does not want the world to know this truth. He will do all he can to stop it and pervert it. Satan is doing a good job of this by spreading and promoting lies.

2 Corinthians 4:4 states, "whose minds the god of this age has blinded, who do not believe, lest the light of gospel of the glory of Christ who is the image of God should shine on them." We live in a generation of people who are being deceived by the gods of this world. They hate and resist followers of Christ and everything Christ followers believe, because they first hated our Savior.

When the situation arises that we feel overwhelmed by these Biblical expectations it is important for us to remind ourselves that we have been given a gift that is beyond measure. Luke 12:48 says, "Unto whom much has been given, much is required." There is no gift more precious, no resource more valuable or life changing than the blood of Jesus Christ that was willingly shed so that we may have eternal life. We are to be: giving, telling, feeding, loving, encouraging and comforting others because of what Jesus did for us. We must share the good news of the gospel! When we are willing and obedient to do this, He will provide what we need to perform it. God has plenty of strength, wisdom and boldness to offer His children.

When moments arise that the sharing of the good news of the gospel seems difficult and intimidating, remember that ultimately it is an honor to be God's servant and to work for the ultimate ruler of the world. It is a gift to know that our Father is *the* answer to life's problems...period!

Since Christians know of this good news, we must share it with the lost world. If God's followers don't do it, who will? Regardless of the problem, we have the answer, Jesus. We cannot keep that answer hidden away.

Think back to when you asked Jesus into your heart to be your savior and the Lord of your life. How did you hear about him? It was because someone shared or sacrificed or committed to and obeyed God so you and I could know of God's great love, His amazing forgiveness and unending power.

If every believer would go to and reach out to the many lost, confused and hurting people around them our world could be changed. When a lost person accepts Jesus and genuinely repents and turns from their old behaviors, they become a testimony to all those who know them.

As children of the Creator of the entire universe, we have been given a priceless gift, one that words can't explain. This is a gift that can't be earned bought or compared to any other gift we have ever been given. Now we are required to share that gift. How and with whom is God asking you to share this gift?

Remember we are all ministers to the lost around us and, we will get tired and possibly consider giving up because it seems too hard, and all hope seems lost. Memorize this verse when those occasions arise Gal. 6:9, "Do not grow weary in doing good, for in due season you <u>will</u> reap what you sow if you faint not." Notice here it says <u>will</u>, not might or possibly, but <u>will</u>. God always keeps his word!

It is obvious that God knows we get tired, and that doing good can wear us out. He knows we get impatient and we sometimes lose hope and we want to give up. He offers encouragement and promise of reward in Revelation 22:12, "And behold, I am coming quickly, and My reward is with Me, to give to every one according to his work." These are promises of rewards to do our Father's work! This is in addition to the gift of eternal life he has already given us. God is truly amazing, nothing compares!

Onward Christian Soldiers

We have just covered some of the expectations God has for us. To help meet those expectations it is up to each of us to work to develop: healthy bodies, minds, spirits, social support and responsibility and financial sensibility. I like to think of this example when I think about developing personal wholeness. If you have ever flown on an airplane, you might remember being told by the stewardess: in the case of an emergency and the oxygen masks are needed, first put yours on then put your children's on. It sounds a bit selfish at first, but in order to help others we have to be sure our foundation is secure and built upon God.

Part II

LET'S GET PRACTICAL

We know wholeness is a beautiful gift from God, by God. This wholeness helps us live for and serve God. Now it is time for each of us to take personal inventory of our lives, and begin our journey towards wholeness.

Chapter 7

THE PHYSICAL COMPONENT OF WHOLENESS

I am not covering the component of physical wellness first because it is the most important. I am covering it first because it is what people notice first when they see us. This component of our humanness also consumes a huge amount of time, thoughts, energy and money. Physical wellness or illness is also the one area of wholeness that most people will talk about more openly.

This openness could be due to the very obvious fact that we human beings all have a visible body. Since we all have a body that is visible and apparent to everyone around us, we are more likely to open up and discuss our physical struggles and frustrations. We aren't so open with our spiritual, mental, financial and social problems. When we look around we can see people struggling with physical challenges and we feel it is safer to share our personal struggles with others when we see theirs.

Another possible factor for more transparency in physical endeavors is because physical issues can be assessed and measured. There is a science to weight control, exercise, flexibility and strength training. These things also respond and change due to our efforts, and these changes are visible to the people around us. Physical activity is something that is doable for almost anyone. It just requires a first step, and all the first step requires is your personal effort. No higher education, no special skill and no financial investment. Although it is a simple principle, it is not an easy principle to follow.

Our bodies have been around since the beginning of time. You would think that since they have been in existence for so long, and because there are so many of them on the road, we would have a little more appreciation of them and treat them a little better. Nevertheless, we watch as people neglect and take their physical bodies for granted. Perhaps people would be a little more interested in taking care of their health if they knew that by developing physical wellness the other areas of their life could be strengthened as well. Look at how physical wellness connects to our social, mental, emotional, spiritual, and financial wellness.

Social wellness

Many individuals who have taken that first step and made physical activity part of their life have found that the *process*, of working towards physical wellness has helped them develop the confidence necessary to take-on and work towards improvement in other components of their wholeness. This positive *process* of engaging in regular physical activity has been so helpful to many people that they in turn want to share that with others. This means that being physically well can help us be socially well because it helps equip us to reach out to others. Notice that I put the word process in italics. This is because the *process* is often more beneficial than the desired outcome alone.

Regular exercise can boost our self confidence, which can also assist with our social wellness because it helps us in approaching and dealing with others. Additional benefits to our social wellness are the numerous social opportunities that present themselves when we go to the gym, tennis court, walking track, basketball court or other group fitness activities.

Interconnection—Our physical wellness can help others. This helping of others is a component of social wellness.

<u>Mental and Emotional wellness</u>

In addition to improving our physical health, exercise has also been shown to posses some therapeutic properties that promote mental and emotional wellness. The benefits are so numerous that the Federal Government is now offering funding to drug and alcohol treatment centers. This money is to be used to develop fitness routines for clients seeking in-patient addiction services.

Other benefits are provided to our mental and emotional health because exercising can provide us with a healthy anger and stress management technique. Cardiovascular exercise can also serve as a natural anti-depressant and helps improve short-term memory. These things will be covered in detail when we discuss mental wellness later in the book.

<u>Interconnection</u>—Physical, mental and emotional wellness.

<u>Spiritual wellness</u>

The most important benefit of physical activity in my life is the way it has drawn me closer to my Heavenly Father. The ability to engage in regular physical activity is a gift and, it provides me with time to talk to my best friend, my Father in heaven.

The time spent running, walking or riding a bicycle is a wonderful time to get alone and focus on and talk to God, or listen to praise and worship music and draw closer to Him. In all honesty, there are many times that I need God's help to get started, and His encouragement and strength to continue on and get through my workout. I am amazed that He cares about this small component of my life and, because He cares it reminds me that although it might be a small component, it is also an important component.

<u>Interconnection</u>—Physical activity can be a functional part of our spiritual development.

Financial wellness

The self discipline that was necessary to start and stick with an exercise routine is definitely useful for our financial wellbeing. This discipline helps us learn to live within our financial means, or better yet, learn to live below our financial means. We must first learn to distinguish the difference between our wants and our needs, and then be able to say no to those wants that exceed our current income level. Frequently our wants are based on the human desire of comfort, ease and enjoyment. None of which are wrong when kept in proper balance. The problem comes when we allow the pursuit of these things to overtake our commonsense and our budget.

A regular physical activity program can help us say no to the fleshly desires of comfort and it can also help us learn to delay gratification, which means we don't get or buy everything we want right now.

Doctors are now saying that regular exercise is one of the most beneficial things people can do for their total wellbeing. The reason being is because those engaged in some type of physical activity greatly reduce their chances of numerous lifestyle diseases including: high blood pressure, high cholesterol levels, stroke, diabetes, various types of cancer, depression and osteoporosis. Preliminary studies are indicating that excessive body fat may contribute to the increase in Alzheimer's disease. Just think about the money saved by avoiding monthly maintenance prescriptions and the necessary doctor visits to regulate and manage them.

Another financial benefit is reported by employers and supervisors who say that their employees who exercise on a regular basis are more efficient at work, have less sick days and qualify for reduced health insurance premiums.

One final benefit offered by taking a step towards and developing an active lifestyle, is that frequently, starting and sticking to an activity program can be the catalyst needed to tackle the more hidden areas of pain and frustration in our lives. As previously stated, it can produce an increase in confidence.

We know beginning a physical activity program is challenging and it requires effort. If it was easy, everyone would be doing it, and health problems would be drastically reduced. So when you begin, no matter how hard it was, remind yourself…you did it anyway! This shows you that you CAN do hard things and it helps prepare you for the future difficulties that <u>will</u> arise.

When a person makes the decision to begin an exercise program and tackles the challenge, they take a very functional step in the right direction towards developing wholeness. When physical wellness is achieved it helps us feel better, when we feel better we are better equipped to face the challenges that accompany life.

<u>Interconnection</u>—Physical, mental, social, spiritual and financial wellness all depend upon and lend support to the others.

God speaks to us by appealing to our physical health

Because God loves us so completely, He cares about our physical wellbeing. God also knows our bodies are important to us and refers to them in His word many times. Frequently disobedience results in negative consequences to our flesh. Deuteronomy 28: 58-62, begins;

"If you do not carefully observe all the words of this law that are written in this book, that you may fear this glorious and awesome name, THE LORD YOUR GOD, Then the Lord will bring upon you and your descendents extraordinary plagues and serious and prolonged sickness. Moreover He will bring back on you all the diseases of Egypt, of which you were afraid, and they shall cling to you. Also every sickness and every plague, which is not written in the book of this law will the Lord bring upon you until you are destroyed. You shall be left a few in number whereas you were as the stars of heaven in multitude, because you would not obey the voice of the Lord your God."

Notice that verse 58 starts with IF, this is God warning His children. In Verse 59 He begins with the word THEN, and He goes on to list the unpleasant consequences, which include sickness and disease. The last verse concludes with: "Because you would not obey the voice of the Lord your God." So the Bible tells us there are physical ramifications for our disobedience.

For our good, God warns us and gives us guidelines to live by; unfortunately we frequently refuse to follow them. We often don't pay attention to the internal non-seen conflicts, or we ignore that still small voice inside of us. Sometimes we turn our heads to the suffering of others, but when the painful things occur in our lives we typically respond. If we don't heed the words of God, He knows how to get our attention. I think C.S. Lewis (Nov. 29, 1898–Nov. 11, 1963) said it best:

"God whispers to us in our pleasures, speaks in our conscience, but shouts in our pains: it is His megaphone to rouse a deaf world."

We know that God is a wise and loving Father and because of this He also blesses our health when we fear, obey and serve him. Proverbs 3:7&8 tells us, "Do not be wise in your own eyes, fear the Lord and depart from evil. It will be health to your flesh, and strength to your bones." Notice it didn't say health to your spirit or strength to your prayer life. He was talking about our bodies.

Look also at Exodus 15:26, "if you diligently heed the voice of the Lord your God and do what is right in His sight, He will put none of the diseases on you which he brought on the Egyptians."

Another promise in regards to physical health and blessings is in Exodus 23:25, "So you shall serve the Lord your God and He will bless your bread and your water, and take the sickness away from the midst of you."

God continually pleas with us to obey Him and promises blessings if we do. Now, I want to very clearly state that I am **not** saying that we obey just to be blessed. If God never does another good thing for any of us, we have all been blessed in more ways than we can comprehend. We obey God because we love Him.

I also am **not** saying that all sickness, disease or injuries are the results of our disobedience. Bad things do happen to good people, and we all live in an imperfect world with imperfect bodies. God originally created a perfect world where all of our needs were met but, when man sinned this perfection was gone, and all of nature was condemned. God put natural principles into place, and when we violate them, there will be negative consequences. Often times, innocent people are victims of these consequences. An example of this is the baby born with severe birth deformities due to a mother's drug use. The Bible tells us there are consequences for disobedience and it also tells us that when we follow the wisdom God offers, the outcomes are much more desirable.

Physical wellness begins on the inside

We have already acknowledged that people in general are more likely to seek help for and discuss physical problems. It is important to know however, that many of the physical problems people seek attention for actually have an internal pathology. A common example of this in our world today is: depression and overeating. Individuals dealing with obesity frequently site depression as a trigger to their overeating. Data provided though a study done by The National Institute of Health showed that both child sexual and physical abuse were associated with a doubling of both depression and obesity when middle age was reached.

Much of our market today tries to cure depression and overeating with physical remedies, prescribing a pill or advising people to just eat less and exercise more, but in reality it is an internal and spiritual healing that is frequently needed. I mentioned food, because food is so readily available and because so many people turn to it. Instead of using food as an example, I could have listed: drugs, alcohol, sex, excessive spending, work, hobbies etc… Everyone has their own *drug* (fix) of choice. Food however is very frequently the Christian's drug of choice.

Another internal and all too common factor in many physical complaints is stress. It is well known that many people experience headaches or anxiety attacks due to excessive amounts of stress. Prolonged stress can also reduce the protective efforts of our immune system, cause a rise in blood pressure and heart rate, contribute to tight muscles, trigger asthmatic attacks, produce tightness in the chest and interfere with a good night's sleep, just to name a few.

The issue is that these things are unseen and can be ignored, denied, suppressed or rationalized, for a while. However, internal crisis will eventually manifest itself through our physical health. The unseen emotional scars, fears, anxiety, addictions, dangerous and destructive thought patterns can be hidden longer and more easily than physical problems, but they will eventually come out. Each of us must pay attention and work towards the development of our unseen components in order to develop and enjoy physical health. These components will be covered in more detail in the chapters dealing with: mental, financial and spiritual wellness.

Chapter 8

THE VALUE OF PHYSICAL WELLNESS

Physical wellness is frequently described as the absence of disease or pain. This is only a portion of the meaning. Physical wellness includes the positive aspects of strength, flexibility, mobility, independence, healthy body weight, the ability to control ones body and its functions and the participation in physical activities with relative ease and no pain. Our bodies are a gift and the ability to move them is also a gift.

How we perceive our bodies can contribute to good health. Wellness demonstrates an attitude that values, respects, nurtures and protects our bodies. It displays the knowledge of knowing when professional medical care is needed, an understanding of the relationship between the need for nutritious food, rest and the necessary daily activities we engage in.

Our bodies are very valuable. The Indiana University School of Medicine conducted a study that suggested the human body had a value of 45 million dollars. Take a look at the price of just a few of our body parts:

Bone marrow—23 million

DNA—1.3 million

Extracting antibodies—7.3 million

The heart—$57,000

2 Lungs—$232,800

2 Kidneys—$ 182,800

Now imagine the rest of all of our body parts, and the valuable fluids in our body needed for life to continue. The surgeon fees, hospital fees, anti-rejection medication and other therapies also need to be added in.

One factor that can't be figured into this 45 million dollar body is the miraculous healing process that God designed and put into operation when He created it. The human body is a magnificent creation. It is so intricate and precise. The design of the human race is not an accident. It is the beautiful and precise creation of the Creator of the universe. Organs, hormones, muscles, neurons, bones, blood, tissues, arms, legs, hands, feet, eyes, ears, fingers, toes, ligaments and tendons all have a specific and necessary function.

The human body still defies modern medicine. Some things still can't be explained by man, and only our Creator himself knows. I think it is interesting to know that as advanced as science and technology have become, they still have not been able to develop a robot that can run like a human being, and they have not yet figured out how to develop blood, there are some things that only God can do.

Another factor to consider when determining the value of our bodies is the fact that God made them with the ability to rebuild and repair themselves. Our physical bodies are very intelligent and they learn how to adapt to the environment around them. How can a price tag be put on this? Look at how we sweat when the temperature rises, consider the automatic processes of digestion, the circulatory system, breathing, adaptations to strength and cardiovascular activities. Our bodies are fighting off infinite free radicals and germs every day. Our hair grows, our skin replenishes itself, our bones rebuild themselves. How can we really assess a value to our bodies and health? I think it is quite fair to say that the health and bodies that God gave us are priceless. There are truly things that money cannot buy.

Additional confirmation of the value of our bodies is found in 1 Corinthians 6:20, "For you were bought for a price, therefore glorify God with your bodies." That price was the highest price anyone could pay, the willing sacrifice of one's life for another. It is important for us to know that God does care about our physical health because He cares about our wholeness, and our physical wellness is a part of this.

Based on what we have just discussed about the value of health, it is baffling that many individuals pay so little time and attention to developing, protecting and nurturing their physical health? Many of us spend more time making sure our cars are running properly, and maintaining adequate fuel, oil and tire pressure levels.

Now, stop and think about the value of the automobile you are maintaining. It is definitely valuable and very important. We all need vehicles to get to work, church, the grocery store and all of our kid's school or sporting activities. Automobiles are a must in today's over scheduled society. The value and importance of vehicles is not in debate. The point is, whether we can find a *running* car that may cost as little as $800. or the more expensive luxury car that can cost as much as a home…. both of these can be replaced. Our bodies however, are the ultimate in automobiles. They are the vehicles that transport us through life, and when they fall apart we have to move out.

Since I brought up automobiles, I'd like to make an analogy. Maybe it will come back to your mind when you need it. Imagine you are putting gas in your car, the tank finally fills up, so you stop. You don't continue pumping and let the gas spill onto the ground. That would be wasteful. The tank is full so there is no need to keep pumping. The next time you are tempted to over eat and finish off the chocolate cake or ice cream in the freezer. Think of your body as the car. The excess food will not simply spill onto the ground, it will spill over onto your hips, thighs, belly, rear-end and double chin….talk about waste. And it is much harder to get rid of the waste on these body parts than it is for the gasoline to evaporate off the ground.

People frequently talk about the value of health, unfortunately most don't pay attention to it until they are sick or injured or struggling with one or more lifestyle diseases. We must all come to know and believe that our bodies and health are valuable, and adopt lifestyles that protect and develop physical wellness. If we say we believe our physical health is important but do nothing to protect or develop it, do we really believe that it is valuable?

If anyone minimizes the gift of being able to move their body and the necessity to do so, they need to talk to someone who is unable to freely move their body or struggling with a debilitating life-threatening disease that has left them bed-ridden, or with a person who is dealing with an illness that requires mega doses of prescription medication, or take the time to consider what it would be like to daily deal with severe chronic pain affecting everything you do. This is not being mentioned to invoke guilt, it is being mentioned so that we learn to appreciate and nurture the gifts that God has given us. It is also not being mentioned to cause anyone to feel depressed or defeated. If you are dealing with chronic pain, a life-style disease, or have been a victim of a disabling accident, there is hope, and engaging in a healthy lifestyle will be beneficial for you as well. Do not focus on the activities you can't do right now. Focus on and do what you CAN do right now. It will lead to more activity and an improvement in your wellbeing over time.

How do we achieve physical wellness?

Physical wellness results from the regular investing of time in the pursuit of healthy eating, development of strength, endurance, flexibility and adequate sleep and hydration. Physical wellness also includes the avoidance of unhealthy habits such as: smoking, illegal drug use, abuse or misuse of prescription medications, excessive drinking of alcohol, excessive eating, sexual activity outside of marriage and the avoidance of excessive stress or the development of an effective stress management plan. It is a simple plan, but it is not always easy to follow.

Physical wellness doesn't happen just by chance or luck and it is not achieved by knowledge alone. Wellness comes through our choices. Most of us know that we need to exercise on a regular basis. We are also aware we need to have an eating plan that is low in fat, sodium and sugar, yet high in fruits and vegetables, along with adequate amounts of lean proteins, complex carbohydrates and water. So, what is stopping us? What keeps us from putting this information to use? What is stopping people from investing a little of their time and self-discipline into something right now that will pay big dividends later? The following chapters will offer specific help with developing a lifestyle that promotes physical wellness.

Deception and physical wellness

Since the human body is valuable and good health is an asset for everyone, everywhere, it is important for us to be aware of the many deceptions, mind-sets, and business practices lurking in every arena of physical wellness that hinder or delay the development of our wellness.

Since each of us is responsible for our thoughts, choices, words and actions, lets first consider the self deception we engage in. Some of these deceptions stop us from making further progress towards total wellness because they can provide a false sense of security, causing us to think that we are fine, therefore no further work is needed. On the other hand, false beliefs can also stop our progress by causing us to feel "there is no use". An example of this is the obese person who concedes to dangerous weight levels because their parents were always overweight.

Notice I used the terms self deception and false belief. This is because these are personal beliefs that are not totally based in truth. They have been adopted by people and have become their reality because they started to believe them. These beliefs have affected their choices. Their choices have shaped their lives and will shape their future.

Beware of body worship

A healthy body that is accompanied by physical strength, endurance and a high energy level is nice and highly coveted by most people. A healthy body however, does not just happen, it requires self discipline, commitment and work. It also sometimes means saying no to things a person really wants like: chocolate donuts, French fries, a double cheeseburger or turtle cheesecake, the list of tempting foods can go on and on. We also have to watch out for the temptation to sleep in late instead of going for that morning run or walk or staying in the comfort of our recliner rather than getting up and getting active.

As important as our bodies and heath are, we must all function in the realization that we are more than just bodies. A body without a mind, will, spirit or emotions is an empty shell. Physically fit individuals know that their bodies are important but, they must be careful not to allow them to become too important. We can make our bodies our idols and we can also become addicted to exercise. Although exercise is a much healthier addiction than cocaine, and it is legal, it can be a life controlling addiction nonetheless. It has the ability to hook, control and consume us, and it can distract us and rob us of the time and energy needed to pursue God's plan for our lives.

If not managed and kept in proper perspective, your workouts can eat away large amounts of time and energy that should be spent with your spouse, children, parents, other family members and friends or at social activities. Working out can also cause problems with work schedules or work performance. Physical activity should definitely be a part of your life, but it should not be your life.

Don't give in

On a regular basis I hear people reconcile themselves to unhealthy lifestyles or chronic diseases because their parents or grandparents struggled with them. Yes I know heredity is a strong factor in many diseases; however genetics is indicated as being thirty percent responsible for this. Our choices are the major force in protecting our health. Maybe your mother was overweight and had high blood pressure and high cholesterol levels because she loved to cook and eat fried foods, and did not get any physical activity. Maybe your father's struggle with an unhealthy level of belly fat is due to over consumption of beer. You do have the choice to eat and drink differently and engage in regular physical activity.

Chronic illness is most often the direct result of poor lifestyle habits. It affects 133 million Americans and causes 7 out of 10 deaths. Chronic illness consumes 2/3 of all money spent on health care in America. More people die every year from lifestyle diseases than the combined total of those dying from drug and alcohol complications.

If you have grown up eating unhealthy foods that are high in fat and sugar it will be difficult to develop a new eating plan. Your body has become addicted to sugar and fat. It has been conditioned to operate on it. You will have the challenging task of re-teaching your body, but it can be done.

Your body and brain can be taught to enjoy and even desire healthy foods like they do the junk food. But it is up to you to be the teacher.

Corporate deceptions

"For the love of money is a root of all *kinds* of evil" (1 Timothy 6:10). Not money itself, but the love of money. Money has way too much power in our world. Many people do very terrible and corrupt things to obtain it. In the industry of human trafficking innocent people are exploited and sold as if they were mere pieces of property, people are murdered for money and countries are betrayed for it. Is it any surprise that big companies will compromise our health for it?

What better way to accomplish this than to sell a product that everyone has to have? Everyone must eat, everyone knows this. Unfortunately many big corporations are more concerned with their profit than they are the health of our country. There are food manufacturers that pay food engineers to develop food that is addictive to humans. Anyone who feels they must have sugar or chocolate to function knows what I'm talking about.

69

A recent study showed that sugar is one of the most addictive foods available, because when it is eaten, chemicals called opiods are released into our brains. This leads to feelings of pleasure, which are similar to the feeling an addict experiences when they ingest their drug of choice. If the sugar is taken away withdrawal symptoms result. Chocolate is another food that affects the brain. This food causes the release of serotonin which actually makes us feel happier.

These food engineers developing these delicious and addictive foods, and big corporate owners profiting from our purchase of them are not concerned with the long term effects their product will have on you or your family's health. They will be retired and jogging on a beach in Rio De'Janerio, while adhering to a very strict organic diet. They are not about to put the junk their company makes in their body.

I don't want to go "conspiracy theory" on you, but who else stands to profit when our health is poor?

—The big pharmaceutical companies. They count on you to continue eating nutritionally poor foods and not taking care of yourself. You get sick and need their medication.

—Doctors who are trained in medical schools funded and controlled by pharmaceutical companies. Doctors and pharmaceutical companies both profit from treating illness and disease, not curing them.

—Insurance companies—In 2009 during a deep economic recession, American health insurance companies increased their profits by 56%, In that same year 2.7 million people lost private coverage.

—The American Cancer Society—The wealthiest non-profit in the world. How many jobs would be eliminated if a cure for cancer was found and made public?

—Weight loss product manufacturers. America is spending more money on these products than ever and yet is now more obese than ever.

—The pink ribbon campaign—This campaign is ran by the Komen Foundation which had assets totaling over $390 million in 2010. Numerous companies, athletes and celebrities don the pink ribbon and make generous cash donations to this campaign. Their main push? Early detection…not prevention. In order to have early detection, expensive screenings are needed, which is a very lucrative means of income. This is an example of big business profiting from the fear and vulnerability of someone's mother, sister or daughter. Also keep in mind, when you give out of the desire to help someone dealing with cancer, only 5.6% of your donation is used to help someone with treatment, and 20.9% goes to fund research. The CEO's salary is $550,000. The Komen Foundation also provides huge amounts to funding to Planned Parenthood, which is the largest abortion provider in the United States.

—Individuals investing in companies that produce junk food and sugary sodas, weight loss products, fitness chains and pharmaceutical companies promising the magic diet pills.

—Although Weight Watchers is a good and healthy program, it and Jenny Craig, Nutri-system and L.A. Weight Loss only stand to benefit from America's obesity epidemic.

It seems like these companies and organizations need help developing Social wellness.

I did not include this section to bash. I simply want you to be aware of what is going on. I encourage you to educate yourself and be proactive about developing and maintaining good health. It infuriates me that big companies are getting rich on the misfortune and suffering of others. But you are not helpless! Your steps towards physical wellness, right now, will profit you. This also profits those who love and need you.

Aside from the financial and physical ramifications of unhealthy lifestyles the most important reason to pursue good health is because God's Word tells us to. I Corinthians 9:27 says, "But I discipline my body and bring it into subjection, lest when I have preached to others I myself should become disqualified." Our physical body is a visual manifestation to the world around us. When properly cared for, it demonstrates that we care about and appreciate our God given and designed bodies. A strong healthy body developed through self-discipline is better equipped to do the work that God has called us to do.

Chapter 9

KNOWLEDGE ALONE DOES NOT EQUAL SUCCESS

With the internet we can look up information about food and exercise anytime. In fact many are self-proclaimed experts in this and other fields because of the readily available cyber technology. But, all the knowledge in the universe is useless if it isn't applied. If all that information stays in our heads but never becomes part of our daily practice, what good is it?

Is it possible that even with the abundance of facts and resources that we still lack a proper appreciation of our bodies? Do we value a big paycheck more than our health? Is temporary comfort more important than a long life of independence and vitality? Do we really believe that a healthy lifestyle is important? If we say we know something and believe it, then why don't we do it? Does this question sound familiar? Is it possible that we really don't believe it is important, or doable or worth the time and effort? Knowing is a great place to start, but it is the doing that bring results.

Since the internet offers users the ability to access a vast amount of information in a matter of seconds, it is a good idea for each of us to do some research on healthy eating and the development of an exercise program. However, it is important to keep in mind that many of the sites are sponsored by a company, physician or fitness guru who has the potential for financial gain, especially if you believe their claims and purchase their product. Give it a try, go to your computer and look up protein drinks, weight loss products or nutritional supplements. Visit several of the sites and see how many of them are hosted by a company who sells these products. Each company will claim that their product is the best and made with only the highest quality and all natural products. Which company claim do we believe?

When checking out products on the internet or other sources, try to find a source of information or website that is generated by an independent research party, company or medical university that merely lists the facts. Facts that are based on research....not profit driven.

To help feed our ever growing appetite for information: books, magazines, television and radio shows featuring information about diet and exercise are abundant. Numerous churches now have weight loss programs. Large and small corporations provide wellness programs for their employees. Even some restaurants have nutrition and exercise tips on their tray liners.

Kids nowadays even know about calories, sugar and fat grams. Back when I was a kid, and I am not saying how long ago that was, but yes we had color television. My friends and I didn't think about how many fat or sugar grams we were taking in. What was a fat gram anyway? We just wanted to down our big glass of kool-aid and eat our cookies as fast as we could so we could go back out to play.

The abundance of information has falsely provided a sense of achievement. Knowledge makes people feel secure and good about themselves. Our society has acquired information, statistics and data, now what? In America there are now more adults and children who are overweight or obese than at any other time in our country. According to the Center for Disease Control, if the current rate of obesity continues in our children, we will have the first generation ever to die younger and sicker than the generation before them. So, the problem is not one due to lack of information, but due to lack of application.

More ignored information

The rate of those who are overweight or obese is so high that it is currently considered a major health crisis. These conditions greatly increase the risk for the following lifestyle diseases: diabetes, heart disease, stroke, some types of cancer, respiratory problems, osteoarthritis, abdominal hernias, varicose veins, dislipidemia, hypertension, sleep apnea, gout, gall bladder disease and liver malfunction.

Once more thanks to technology, these lifestyle diseases and high obesity levels are widely known about by most people. We are aware of methods to prevent or control these diseases, but for some reason a large percentage of Americans are not acting on this startling information. Perhaps, rather than learning and storing up more information we should learn more about ourselves, and what we are allowing to stop us from actively responding to this information.

One more component that needs to be considered in regards to obesity is the financial ramifications of this lifestyle disease. In America 190 billion dollars were spent in medical care for obesity related health problems, individuals who are obese spend on average $1850.00 more per year than those who are average weight. America as a nation helped the weight loss industry gain a 60.9 billion dollar profit, by purchasing their gimmicks, gismos and fad diet plans. Yet in spite of the tremendous amount of money spent to fight the battle of the bulge, the overweight and obesity rates are still reaching historically high levels. No amount of money can make healthy food choices or exercise for us. In order for us to enjoy the benefits of physical wellness it is imperative for us to live a healthy lifestyle....for the rest of our lives.

Let me tell you something that sounds obvious, and will save you some money. This fact seems foreign to many. Some people know it, but don't want to believe it. OR, just don't really want to adhere to it. To lose weight you MUST burn more calories than you take in! It is a fact, it is a mathematical principle. No expensive personal trainer, diet pill, fat burner or fat blocker can change that. It is a very simple principle, but not a principle that is easy to apply. Save your time reading, researching and trying to find the right pill. Start putting what you know to work. Right now, just start moving your body and develop an eating plan that benefits your health, for life.

One final point before closing this chapter, I think it is imperative to acknowledge that obesity is a dynamic condition. It is not a condition that responds to physical actions alone. Obesity is a symptom that usually has an internal non–physical origin.

Interconnection. When dealing with obesity the entire (whole) person must be considered.

**** *There are some medical conditions and medications that lead to weight gain. It is important to discuss this with your doctor so they can help you address all medical concerns.*

That being said, it is still important for everyone to develop and follow a healthy eating and physical activity program. Thyroid disorders, and many other disorders that cause weight gain respond very well to the development of a healthy lifestyle.

Chapter 10

EATING FOR WELLNESS

We have determined what wholeness is, why it is important and how it includes the physical seen components and also the non-seen components of the whole person. It is time to look at and apply healthy and practical principles in our choices. If we are what we eat, what are you?

Food and eating are both necessary. Herein lies a great conundrum. The Food that we all strive for because it is necessary for us to live, is the same thing that can rob us of the very thing we are trying to preserve. Food provides many benefits and at the same time causes numerous problems for us. Since we have to eat to survive, wise food choices are important to all of us.

Develop an eating plan that benefits you for life

A healthy eating plan that you can follow for life is a plan that needs to be developed by you. Help is available if needed, and a Physician, Dietician or Weight Loss Specialist can assist you in the development of a healthy and nutritious eating plan. The key to it working and being effective for you, is your willingness to follow it.

You are more likely to follow a eating plan that you research and develop. Who knows you better than you? Who has lived in your body with your mind longer than you? You know the food you like and those you don't, and the foods you might like but don't like you. You know your budget and schedule. Develop a plan that works for you and one that you WILL follow.

Review the standard food pyramid, which can be found on the internet or by going to your local library. It has been around many years and it is safe, sound and simple. Identify how many servings of protein, carbohydrates, dairy products and produce you need each day. Make a commitment to stick to eating these recommended servings on a regular basis. Making healthy choices frequently and consistently enough for an extended amount of time will make healthy eating a habit. If you make healthy eating choices long enough, those cravings for high fat and sugar foods will be reduced and believe it or not you can actually train yourself to enjoy healthy foods like fruits and vegetables but, it does take time. Stop and look at how many years you have fed your body unhealthy and nutritionally empty foods. It will be an adjustment, but it can happen.

There will be days when you don't eat enough protein, or produce. There will be days when you eat too many chocolate chip cookies or have second or third helpings at dinner and there will be days when you don't get up in time to exercise. That is life, and life happens. Do not get discouraged and give up! Just start over and make it a point to make healthy choices more often than you make unhealthy choices. Remember the development of wellness is a journey, and with every journey there are delays, wrong turns, bad directions and bad drivers who get in our way. Consider this; if you were going on a trip and you discovered that you took a wrong turn, you would (hopefully) stop and turn around and go in the right direction. You wouldn't say, oh well I took a wrong turn I guess I'll just keep going in the wrong direction.

A healthy life style should be pursued in the same manner. If you make a wrong choice stop right there turn around and go in the right direction of building and striving for wellness. Again, it is a process and it takes time. One bad choice will not destroy the results of several good choices, just like one good week of eating right and exercising will not change 10 years of being inactive and living on junk food.

Food is supposed to be nourishment for our bodies. It is designed to help them grow, heal and be active. Food is not the enemy! It is the misuse of and excessive intake of food that becomes the problem. We would be wise to take the emotion and moralization out of food. It is helpful to think of food in economical terms. We want to make wise purchases and wise investments with our money. We want to get the most out of our buck. We want security for our future, and funds to not only live on but have fun with. All of these are good desires. What if we thought about food that way? Make your food choices work for your body and for your future. Get the most nutrition you can out of your food.

Make it a family affair

There are many nutritionally sound eating plans available. When designing yours it is important to find one that not only you like and will follow, but also your family likes. Wellness should be a family affair. Fixing two different menus will become very tiresome and it can get complicated buying two different types of foods. Remember this is not a diet, but a plan, and everyone needs the opportunity to provide feedback. Keeping junk food in the house because your children or spouse want it is just a temptation that doesn't have to be, and your family members don't need junk food anymore than you do. There are just so many times a person can say no to those cookies you bought or those cupcakes that were baked, "just for the kids", or the brownies or chocolate cake sitting on the counter. If it isn't in front of you, it is not visually tempting you every time you walk by, and better yet, if it is not in the house the temptation is tremendously reduced. This step of keeping temptation out of our homes, offices, computers and automobiles can be useful in numerous situations, not just healthy eating.

The wonderful taste of many junk foods is temptation enough but, it is also readily available everywhere we go. Plates of freshly baked cookies are set on the table at meetings. Boxes of donuts set out in the conference room at work, or on the table at the back of your Sunday school class, pretty dishes of candy are on everyone's desks and vending machines are stocked with chips and candy bars. It would be a wise move to plan ahead and keep nutritionally sound food choices on hand to replace junk food with healthy choices when you can, or better yet don't eat anything unless you are experiencing stomach hunger. Even then it is fine to experience hunger on occasion.

When developing a healthy eating plan with your family it will be easy to be led astray by fad diets. There are diets out there that will help a person lose weight. Yes, if you eat only lettuce every day, you will lose weight. But is that a nutritious eating plan? Where is the protein that is necessary for tissue growth and repair? Where is the calcium for healthy teeth and bones? Eating lettuce will lead to weight loss, but physical wellness goes far beyond just a number on the scale or a pant size. Besides how long could you really stick to a diet of only lettuce? Again, choose and build an eating plan that benefits your body for life. Don't diet, develop!

We have previously acknowledged that our bodies are the temple of the Holy Spirit and we are to honor God with them. Remind yourself and your family of this when developing your family eating plan. Our bodies are a precious and valuable gift from God. He designed them so precisely, and He is loaning them to us for our use while we are on this earth. A healthy eating plan is important because it is an essential component of nurturing and fueling our bodies. When we take care of this temple we are being faithful stewards with one of the many precious resources God has given us.

A healthy eating plan is a balancing act

It is no secret that our country has a multi-trillion dollar deficit right now, and if the trend continues it will grow even larger. This scares the citizens of our country and those of the many other countries who have been helped by America. It is a very bad position to be in, but in terms of weight control creating a deficit is a good thing. It is just too bad that it takes so much more effort to create a calorie deficit than is does to create a financial deficit.

The easiest and most effective way to create this deficit is through the combination of a healthy eating plan (one you can follow for life) and regular physical activity. The combination of reducing calorie intake and increasing physical activity <u>will</u> produce results if done long enough, frequently enough and at the right intensity. It is not a trick, and it is not always easy. If it was easy and convenient, everyone would be doing it and the diet and medical industries would go bankrupt.

A study completed by the National Weight Control Registry showed that individuals who participated in a weight loss program that combined healthy eating with regular exercise were more successful at losing weight and keeping it off. These people also expressed more ease at weight loss than those who used either calorie restriction or exercise alone.

This goes back to economy (physical not financial), and learning how to burn more than we take in. In addition to increased activity and decreased calories, another way to create a deficit is to reduce the amount of time spent in sedentary activities. We all should get up and move during commercials or, stand up and walk while talking on the phone. If possible do not sit in front of the computer for more than one hour at a time. We know the other recommendations: park farther away from the store, take the stairs when possible, walk to do errands, take your dog for a walk or go visit your neighbor instead of calling them.

Losing weight is a challenge, in fact to lose just one pound, a person must burn 3,500 calories more than they take in. This also applies to gaining one pound, which requires an extra intake of 3,500 calories. So that Snickers bar did not cause you to gain five pounds, and going for a 30 minute walk will not make you lose it. The number 3,500 sounds pretty daunting. However, if it is divided by seven it actually translates into creating a 500 calorie per day deficit.

As previously stated, it is best to create this deficit through the combination of a sensible eating plan and regular physical activity. This can be done by reducing your daily calorie intake by just 250 and increasing you activity level to burn off an extra 250 calories per day. What does this looks like in real life? Go for a three mile (brisk) walk, and cut your soda in-take down from three to just one per day. Another example to consider, participate in an aerobic or martial arts class and choose two pieces of cheese pizza on thin crust instead of three or four pieces of supreme and use reduced fat dressing for your salad. Reduced fat dressing is suggested instead of fat free because some fat is needed to help with the processing of the fat soluble vitamins A, D, E & K and numerous other physiological functions.

Figure out your daily calorie budget

If your goal is to lose weight, it is important to determine how many calories (dollars) you need each day. Just like money, you need to keep track of the calories you spend or take in each day. Basically figure out a food and activity budget. It doesn't have to be extremely regimented, but it does need to be balanced and it must be followed....at least the majority of time. Numerous websites are available to help you figure our your daily caloric need based on your: gender, age, height, current weight and activity level.

Determining your caloric need will help prevent the temptation to follow severe calories restriction or crazy fad diets. My personal opinion is that a 1,200 calorie diet is too low for women and 1800 calories per day is too low for men. A person can follow it for a period of time and will lose weight. But, what happens when the calorie consumption rises back to the normal 2200-3000 calories per day? The weight will return. A healthy eating plan is all about moderation, and developing eating habits that benefit you for life. Remember you are embarking on a journey, a journey towards wellness that will last a life time. What good is a diet that you can't follow for life and be healthier by it?

I used the term calories, some people don't like that term and would rather refer to it as points. While the majority of food products have calories listed on their labels, some are now listing points in addition to calories. This is good and it provides another way to be aware of what and how much we are taking in.

Keep a food journal

Once a calorie or point limit is determined a food journal is a very helpful tool. This journal is a good way to clearly identify how much you eat, and help identify triggers that contribute to overeating. Many of us snack and eat without being mindful of it or how much we have eaten. We also tend to eat when we are not hungry. We eat when we are bored, tired, lonely, when we want to celebrate, when we watch television or just for the fact that food is around and it tastes and smells so good.

This food journal is for your eyes only, unless you have an accountability partner, trainer or dietician you want to discuss it with. Write down what you eat, where you are when you eat it and how much. It helps keep you accountable, and it provides a means to help identify problem foods and triggers. A food journal also helps you see how quickly and easily the calorie count can rise. Sometimes just the process of having to write everything down stops people from eating when they are not hungry.

When beginning your food journal write down everything that goes into your mouth. Don't minimize, just report honestly. Remember, no one has to see this journal unless you want to show them. If you have cream and sugar with your coffee, be sure to write down how many teaspoons you use of each. If you have a salad write down how much dressing, cheese, bacon, nuts or ham you put on the salad. Some restaurants offer salads that have up to 2,200 calories. You would have been better off ordering that burger you really wanted. With this in mind, it is important for you to take the time to educate yourself before you eat out, and know what you are putting into your body. Many restaurants now have their menu on-line. Check it our before you head out the door. Seemingly healthy food choices at some restaurants can turn out to be a nightmare to your healthy eating.

If you have a dish of Hershey's kisses or jelly beans on your desk be sure to keep track of how many you eat....don't just guess. All the small things do add up, and are often over looked. Sodas, shakes, protein drinks, energy drinks, milk, kool-aid, fruit juice and alcoholic beverages all count too, and many people overlook this.

Remember your food journal does not have to be kept indefinitely or in some fancy computer program or leather journal. Keep it simple and convenient. It is important to document your intake on weekdays **and** weekends, because we tend to eat differently on the weekend.

Through the years of personal training, the majority of those I have trained want to lose weight and, most of these clients claimed they ate very little. This cannot be the case, unless there is some medical condition. To help identify problem eating, I suggest that they keep a food journal like the one previously described. To their surprise after just a week of keeping this journal they were able to see where modifications needed to be made, and they become aware of portion sizes, eating triggers and mindless and emotional eating.

The purpose of the food journal is not to make you neurotic, or to add just one more event to your already cram-packed schedule. It is merely to make you aware of everything you put into your mouth. By becoming more mindful about when, where, why and how much we eat, we become more equipped to make healthier eating choices.

The food journal is a tool and it provides one more source of information. Remember though, information and tools without application are useless. Once you have more tools and information it is up to you to put them to use on your journey towards physical wellness.

Become a label reader

Many people have become label readers. This is progress, and it is great. It is important though to read the entire label. Not just the calorie count. It is important to know what a serving size is. People tend to confuse portion sizes with the suggested serving size.

I see this frequently while having clients complete an eating assessment. Individuals will state that they have one or two sodas per day. With a bit of investigating, I found out that these were 20 ounce bottles which actually turned out to be five servings when drinking two of them. This is double what they thought.

Also look at cereal boxes, a serving size can be ½ cup up to a whole cup. Until I took the time to read this, a full bowl was a serving in our house. When I figured this out I saw that what we were eating when filling our bowl was actually three servings, pretty disturbing. I still often wonder if any one really gets full on ½ cup of cereal. Better yet check out Doritos, just nine chips make a serving. Can anyone really stop at just nine Doritos? My biggest disappointment came when I read that a box of Crunch & Munch actually has three servings, really? I can easily and quickly eat a whole box myself, and still want more. I don't buy that snack anymore.

Our society has become used to supersized everything, but we can train our bodies to become satisfied with less food. This does take time, practice and commitment. This was previously mentioned when speaking about teaching your body to enjoy and crave healthy food. This education of your body is done through exposing and ingesting healthy food in the right amounts on a regular basis.

Once you have read the calorie count, recommended serving size and nutrition information, be sure to check out the ingredients list. The first ingredient listed is the one with the highest percentage in the food. I.E. wheat bread is often just white bread with caramel coloring added. Make sure the first ingredient listed is whole wheat.

Avoid diets that eliminate one food group

God gave us a variety of foods with fantastic and different tastes, smells and textures. If food was only for the meeting of nutritional needs, God could have easily provided just one food with one taste to meet that basic human need. God, however, is so creative and generous that He loves to provide for and offer delight to His children. Food can be a great source of enjoyment. The problem comes when food becomes our only source of enjoyment and we use it excessively to fill in other areas of our lives where we might be experiencing lack.

The problem with weight gain is not from a certain food, the problem comes when we go overboard with that food, or we misuse food. One or two pieces of pizza can be part of a healthy eating plan. When we start eating five or six pieces of pizza that is going overboard, and it is no longer a stomach hunger that is driving us to eat but something else.

I like the verse in I Corinthians 6:13, "Foods for the stomach and stomach for foods, but God will destroy both it and them. Now the body is not for sexual immorality but for the Lord, and the Lord for the body." Food is meant to go into the stomach to be digested to help our bodies heal and develop. It is a basic human need, however, isn't it wonderful to know that God made food something we could enjoy to meet this basic need. What if it was like medicine? Our appetites for food are God given, the problem comes when they control us and we don't control them. Appetites can apply to any desires in our lives, not just food.

Food is not designed to be our companion in helping us overcome loneliness, it is not designed to be an anxiety or stress reliever, it is not meant to be a cure for boredom. I like how God uses the correlation in the verse above, food is for the stomach and stomach for foods, and then it goes on to say, the body is not for sexual immorality, but for the Lord, and the Lord for the body. The most powerful part of that verse is the last five words "*The Lord for the body.*" God is for us, He cares about every part of us, even our bodies. Yes, our bodies may be perishing daily, but that doesn't mean to ignore, abuse, misuse or neglect them. We also shouldn't idolize them or let the pursuit of the perfect body replace the pursuit of seeking, serving, trusting in and striving to honor our Heavenly Father.

If you have a food allergy, or your doctor has advised you to avoid a certain food group then obviously some foods must be eliminated. However, for the average individual most foods can be enjoyed in the right amounts. Some of these wonderful foods should be enjoyed a little less than others.

Carbohydrates are not bad

I get so frustrated when I hear people say they quit eating carbohydrates. This is an unnecessary sacrifice and it has been promoted by many people…even doctors.

If you *overeat* carbohydrates, which is easy to do because they are so abundant and they taste so fantastic, you will gain weight. If you quit ingesting excessive calories you will lose weight. In all my years of training I have seen many people lose weight by swearing off carbohydrates, but I have as of yet to see any of them maintain this loss by avoiding carbohydrates. I'm not saying these people don't exist, I'm just saying I don't know any of them.

Please keep this in mind, carbohydrates provide B vitamins, they are a major source of energy, especially for the brain and nervous system and they help maintain the healthy functions of the organs. They erroneously get a bad rap. One of the problems with carbohydrates is they taste so good. It is very easy to overeat brownies, chips, cookies, donuts, ice cream, pastries or French fries, but how often does a person over eat spinach or broccoli? In addition to tasting so good, another consideration to look at is the fact that many carbohydrates also have a high fat content or they are topped or prepared with fatty or high sugar food products.

Look at endurance athletes like: runners, bikers, tri–athletes, swimmers. The majority of their calories (60%–70%) come from carbohydrates, why aren't they overweight? Oh yeah, I know…. because they are so active. Most of us don't have the time, or desire to swim, run or bike three to five hours per day, but we also would not need to take in 3000–5000 calories per day as some of these athletes do. So please remember you do not have to eliminate carbohydrates to maintain a healthy body weight. For some of you who have been torturing yourself, it was worth it to buy this book just to read that.

There is one caveat; all carbohydrates are not created equal. Make sure your carbohydrate choices are complex carbohydrates. Like: brown rice, whole grain pasta, whole wheat bread, millet, oats, wheat germ, barley, wild rice, buckwheat, oat bran, cornmeal, beans, peas, quinoa, couscous, popcorn (air popped) and amaranth. Most vegetables and some fruits are also complex carbohydrates, and are high in water, vitamins and fiber content while being virtually fat-free.

The reason simple carbohydrates like white flour, bread, pasta and white rice should be replaced by complex carbohydrates is because the simple carbohydrates are more processed and are less healthy, this is because the outer and inner germ layer have been removed from the original kernel. This allows the simple carbohydrate to be more quickly absorbed, resulting in a higher glycemic index. This is what causes a spike in blood sugar levels. Remember the phrase; what goes up must come down. When our blood sugar drops we can get groggy, irritable or even depressed, this leads us to seek more simple carbohydrates. And the cycle continues, this is one ride you need to get off of.

The misrepresentation and negative rap that carbohydrates get is a very unnecessary frustration for many people. It has been advertised and discussed so much that many truly believe they have to eliminate carbohydrates from their diet in order to lose weight. This is incorrect!

Too many calories and not enough physical activity are the causes of most weight gain. Carbohydrates in and of themselves are not bad. In fact, the Bible frequently speaks about carbohydrates. No, the Bible does not use that word, but it does speak of bread 360 times. I'm not trying to prove a theological principle here, just wanted you to reconsider your stance if you are experiencing a carbohydrate phobia.

Jesus called himself the *Bread of Life, in* John 6:35. In Luke 22:1-23, at the last supper Jesus used bread to symbolize his body, why didn't he use meat; wouldn't that have been a better representation of flesh? The Manna that God used to feed the Israelites was a type of carbohydrate. Another reference to carbohydrates is the miracle of Jesus multiplying the fishes AND the loaves. Would Jesus multiply something that was harmful for his children? No, His plans, provisions and commands are for our safety and good. What we have done is over processed, misused and abused these carbohydrates like most of the other beautiful gifts that God has given us.

Fat doesn't make you fat

Our bodies need fat. But once more our problem comes with excess. Fat is necessary for the process of fat soluble vitamins, and it insulates our bodies, and organs. The type of fat (much like carbohydrates) is what we need to pay attention to. In general, fat coming from plant sources like nuts and avocados is good fat. Fat coming from animal sources, whole milk, meats, fried foods, chips, cookies and cakes is unhealthy. The exception to this is the omega-3 fat found in some fish. It is a good and necessary type of fat. Red meat can also be part of a healthy diet, just make sure lean cuts are purchased and visible fat is trimmed or drained off.

Fat is not bad on our bodies either, again it is when we carry excessive fat around with us. Just as having too much body fat is unhealthy, being skinny is not always a guarantee of good physical health. I have administered close to 2,000 fitness assessments on gym members. I have lost track of how many skinny people I met with who were unable to complete the brief 15 minute fitness assessment either because they got tired and couldn't finish the cardiovascular portion of the test or they did not have the strength to complete the strength portion of the test. On the other hand, I have also had some muscle heads that breezed by the strength portion of the test but, were unable to finish the cardiovascular portion of the assessment and failed the flexibility test.

When seeing skinny people walk into a gym, I have heard numerous people say something like "that person is skinny, they don't need to be here." We are not going for skinny! Remember skinny doesn't always transpire into total wellness.

Stay away from ALL diet pills

Many individuals have lost weight by using diet pills that suppress the appetite. The problem is that the majority of these individuals do not keep the weight off once the diet pill is discontinued.

The appetite is something that is very human. God gave it to us to keep us alive, to help us survive. In the long run it is much, much, more healthy to learn to deal with the appetite than it is to take pills that suppress it or give us energy while stimulating and raising our heart rates. Yes, diet pills are easier, for the here and now, but we are going for a lifetime of physical wellness. What good does it do to waste six months or even two weeks on an unsafe fad diet or diet pill? That is six months or two weeks that you will never get back. It is good to eat when you are hungry, that is what the appetite is for. It is also good to STOP eating when our stomachs are full. It is not good to use food as an anti-depressant, a friend, a pain reliever or to cure boredom, loneliness or anxiety.

Sometimes we eat just because food looks good, it smells good, everyone else is eating or just because its there. Food is wonderful, I love it, and I look forward to eating, and sometimes I over do it. At one time or another all of us have over eaten or indulged in high fat or high sugar foods. This is allowable occasionally, as long as 85-90% of our choices are nutritionally sound and promote the functions of our bodies. I was happy to find that even the Bible says that it is o.k. to eat junk food on occasion. Nehemiah 8:10 states, "Then he said to them 'Go your way, eat the fat, drink the sweet and send portions to those for whom nothing is prepared'."

Interconnection—Every action/choice or emotion starts with a thought, which means that new thoughts and beliefs can lead to new behaviors. Unhealthy thoughts about food and eating are a habit, and its time to start breaking that habit. Try to start looking at food as a necessary element to your productiveness and you might just find it a little easier to control what goes in your mouth. Start right now by telling yourself "I eat to live, I don't live to eat" Take the first step towards controlling your food intake by reviewing your personal perspective on food and eating. It will be difficult, most worth while endeavors are. Remember you are introducing yourself to a new way of living.

Supplementation

It is my opinion that when a person has a well balanced eating plan, with plenty of fruits and vegetables, adequate protein, complex carbohydrates, water and proper rest, supplements are not needed. I know however, there are some individuals who have been told by their physician to supplement their diet with vitamins. I am NOT advising you against their medical advice. If it works for you and you are getting good results you need to continue on.

If there is a food group you can't eat or won't eat, or you engage in strenuous, high intensity physical activity, you may need supplements to insure that your body gets the vitamins, minerals, anti-oxidants, fiber and protein it needs. If you have always taken vitamins and that is part of your daily routine, I am not telling you to quit. Most vitamins taken as directed are safe. However, if you are eating, exercising and sleeping like you should, while eliminating unhealthy lifestyle choices the vitamins you are purchasing might be an unnecessary expense.

Supplements are man made based on man's wisdom. As vast and advanced as this wisdom might be, the closer we can stay to nature, God's original design, the better off we will be. The processing of foods significantly reduces their nutritional values, and often adds unnecessary sodium, sugar, fat, flavorings and chemical additives.

Chapter 11

MOVE IT, MOVE IT, MOVE IT!

Our bodies were made to move, and they perform better and last longer when we move them on a regular basis. Yet why do so many people avoid exercise and activities that require physical exertion? The excuses are numerous. Some are a bit legitimate, but largely I believe our decision to follow through on the incorporation of regular physical activity into our lives stems from what is important to us. Is it just possible that we don't truly appreciate and value our bodies and physical health as we should?

There are various road blocks to getting active. These road blocks can have roots in many different variables. Most of them are highly effective in throwing us off the path towards wellness because they shape our perception of exercise.

A very common road block preventing many people from developing a fitness routine is based on past unsuccessful experiences with physical activities. Like in childhood P.E. class. Remember the sit-ups with someone sitting on our feet, the jumping jacks and toe touches, or the pull-ups for the boys and the arm hangs for girls. Personally I thought that was miserable, it was not something that I looked forward to. It really was not fun....it was a chore and even humiliating. Who wants to engage in activities that humiliate them? None of us likes to do things that we are bad at. Almost all of us avoid the possibility of failure or ridicule, but by continually avoiding failure and ridicule we are indirectly passing by our opportunity for success and good health.

Others may avoid sports or recreational activities because of a malicious bully in that P.E. class who ridiculed them when they tried to participate in sports or physical activities. How about always being picked last when teams are being formed? This makes people feel that they are bad at athletic activities, or any physical activity for that matter. Again, this is not something any of us would consider enjoyable.

Now hear this!

That bully is gone. Do not let him live rent free in your brain any more. Your past attempts (not failures) at physical activity can be learning tools to help you develop a personal activity program that you can succeed at and enjoy now. All it takes is a little time, big commitment and a concerted effort to do this, no financial investment or special skill required.

If your past experience with physical activity was made overly difficult due to health or physical limitations, perhaps you don't think the discomfort or effort is worth it. To those dealing with asthma; running or vigorous cardiovascular activity is not something they look forward to. Breathing is pretty important and something I've come to value. Young athletes injured by overzealous coaches also tend to dislike or approach activity tentatively. It doesn't have to be this way. An effective fitness program is safe and one that you can follow for life. Everyone does not have to run, or play football or become a body builder, just learn to move your body in some way everyday.

A false perception that prevents people from exercising is the belief that physical activity is only for athletes. Not true! Years ago my children and I were out playing softball....just for fun and to get out of the house. I say this because none of us had actually played on a real softball team. We invited a young neighbor boy to play with us. He declined at first, saying "we aren't athletes in my family". After much persuasion he gave in and joined us. It took numerous pitches before he made contact with the ball, but he finally did and got to run the bases. He actually ended up having fun and asked if we could play again the next day. That neighbor boy is now an active member of an athletic team at his local high school.

God made our bodies to move. Exercise or physical activity is like every other endeavor we begin. It is difficult at first, but the more we do it the easier it gets and the better we get at it. Be willing to try again regardless of past attempts. Don't give up too soon, progress takes time.

Another barrier to getting active is experienced by those who are dealing with being overweight or obese. The physical struggle from the extra weight they are carrying stops them from attempting physical activity, either because it is just too difficult, the weight may actually cause pain or due to fear of public criticism. Getting active is not easy, but it is absolutely necessary.

If you are dealing with excessive weight right now, remember that is a temporary number and it will only change if your choices change. The weight you are carrying can and will be reduced if you start and stick with a wellness plan. It is up to you. Regardless of past choices, attempts, mistakes and hurts, you can have wellness now. Your past is only part of you. Your future is yours to grasp and shape. Take control of it right now, no more lost time. Remember "If you want different results, you must take a different approach."

The most sited reason for not exercising is lack of time. Our world is so rushed and the average family is over scheduled. Our jobs take the bulk of our day. Then we have homes, children and yards to take care of, meetings, practices and church to attend. Each of us has 24 hours to invest, and it is important to be intentional about how we invest our time. We must all take a personal inventory and determine what is most important in our lives. Is it really important for our children to participate in a sporting or other type of competitive event every night? Is it really necessary to work 50-60 hours every week? Is it helpful to sit in front of the television and flip through the channels for an hour, or sit in front of the computer and view what everyone had for dinner on their Facebook posts? Outside of work, most of our time is ours; we make the decision to whom or what we will give it.

What is holding YOU back?

Whether it is a lack of time or past painful or unsuccessful experiences that are causing you to avoid any physical endeavors, it is now time to begin. Whatever barrier(s) is/are stopping you from working towards developing a well lifestyle, tear it or them down now. None of us can do anything about the past....not one single thing, it cannot be changed! However we can learn from it, and decide to stop allowing it to stand in our way.

Today, you can start working to build a new future and a stronger, healthier body. The only person, thought or criticism stopping you is yours. There is only one you, take care of you! When you feel discouraged, overwhelmed or unable to take steps towards getting active, draw back to your remembrance

2 Corinthians 9:8, "And God is able to make all grace abound toward you, that you, always having all sufficiency in all things, may have an abundance for every good work." Getting active is a good work.

It starts in your head

We have previously acknowledged that our attitudes and beliefs determine our choices. In our modern society, the media plays a huge role in determining our attitudes. The next time you see or hear of a diet, weight loss product or exercise gimmick stop and see if that advertisement says something like, "*I lost 50 pounds without ever stepping into the gym*" or "*lose weight without ever sweating.*" Some commercials even call exercise *grueling.* That really makes a person get excited about exercise. Other diet pill endorsements talk as if exercise is punishment or the price someone has to pay to be lean and healthy.

We should look at and think about the ability to move our bodies under our own volition as a gift. The ability to control, move and push our bodies is a phenomenon made possible through God's magnificent and articulate design of the muscles, joints, bones, nerves, heart and lungs. Our body is a precious gift and moving it is a great way to preserve it.

An effective way to get moving and to change our moods and actions is to first work on changing our thoughts and beliefs. Say to yourself, I CAN do it, I WILL do it and it is IMPORTANT! Say it over and over again, until you believe it. No, it definitely is not easy. There are some days the minutes or the miles or the repetitions crawl by, but isn't life like that at times? I like to think of a daily exercise session as practice for life. Sometimes you feel tired...do it anyway. Sometimes you want to quit....you can't quit, life goes on. Sometimes you climb a hill while running and you feel like your legs are on fire, that helps prepare you for life and the difficult situations that feel like an endless uphill climb. Lift heavy things, attempt difficult things, be willing to mess up and keep trying until you get it. This might present itself in the form of learning to do a push up or running your first mile.

I know of a woman who was a smoker and also spent 16 years dealing with an eating disorder, and had some physical problems, and emotional issues from these years of struggle, she told me that she frequently thought of suicide because she felt there was no hope of recovery for her. She tried out-patient counseling, anti-depressants, support groups and even went to a 30 day treatment center. One spring she heard that a 5k run was being held in her town for a charity she cared deeply about. She began running a short distance...mostly walking at first.

In time she was able to run up to five miles without stopping. When looking back to how her running began, she told me that the first day she began running was the first healthy eating day she had in 16 years, and that was also the day that she quit smoking. Her depression was also lifted. The success she experienced from tackling and sticking with a running program gave her confidence and the drive to go back to college and finish her degree. She praises God for giving her the gift of physical activity and delivering her from a life threatening eating disorder, helping her become smoke free, strengthening and conditioning her to face difficult things and go back to college after being out for 20 years.

When we make the decision to take a step towards wellness, we have made a very important and beneficial decision. It all starts with a decision. Our thoughts and beliefs have a very powerful impact on our choices and behaviors. Exercise is a physical activity but it begins with an invisible mental activity, a personal decision. Making this decision on a regular basis, whether you feel like it or not is self-discipline. This self discipline not only helps you get into a fitness routine, it shows that you can make yourself do things that are difficult. It shows that you do have control over your health and the rest of your life as well.

Physical activity can help improve your mind-set for the day. If you schedule it early in the morning, you can consider your first task for the day completed! Exercise is a good investment of your time, and it all started with your decision, even if it was a hesitant and much debated decision.

There are many times I have regretted how I spent my time, but I have never regretted time spent running, lifting weights or going for a walk with my husband, playing ball or riding bikes with my kids or talking with God while I am out on my run. I have to remind myself of this frequently because; many times it is very difficult to get started. I am just not looking forward to sweating and breathing hard and every part of me is saying no! My body is saying, just sleep in a little later, my mind is telling me; you really don't have time to exercise, you have too much to do. However, when I make the decision to start, and then complete my workout, I am always glad I did it. You will be too....in time, and after the initial soreness wears off.

I was recently talking with a pastor who runs. We were talking about how difficult it is to motivate yourself when schedules get overloaded and the summer heat index reaches 105°. Honestly, there are even days with perfect temperatures that require a pep talk to get me out the door. This preacher made a statement that I like to recall when I am dreading or avoiding my run. He said he thinks of running as a dying to the flesh. What a realistic analogy. Sometimes I feel like I might die while I'm running. But I'm always glad when I finish.

Need more encouragement? Take the time to talk to people who have engaged in some type of physical activity on a regular basis, over an extended amount of time. Listen to how their increase in activity levels has made the physical tasks that used to tire them out a little easier. Listen to how it has improved their mood and sleep and how their energy levels have increased. Talking to people who are active can help adjust your beliefs about exercise and offer encouragement to help you get started. Weight loss is also a benefit that many active people are happy to talk about.

One last thought about exercise, and I think this is very valuable. You have control of it! No one can exercise for you. If they do, they get the benefit not you. You can control how long you walk or run, you can decide if you are doing 10, 12 or 15 repetitions. Your physical health as an adult is your responsibility, and sometimes starting with the development of physical wellness gives us strength and confidence to tackle the mental, spiritual, social and financial development of our lives.

Forget that boring P.E. class! There are tons more ways to exercise than doing chin-ups, sit-ups and jumping jacks. Just get moving! Get outside and enjoy nature, take your dog for a walk, turn on your favorite music and dance in the middle of your living room. Go rake your neighbor's yard, shoot some hoops, get out and ride the bike that has been hidden in the garage for three years, play catch with your children, or some of the neighborhood kids, start training for a local 5k charity walk or run, take tennis lessons, join an adult ball team or cycling club, go to the local walking trail. Some video stores, like Family Video actually rent out exercise videos free of charge. The opportunities are vast, just get started, and move it, move it, move it!

Chapter 12

WHAT CONSTITUTES A WORKOUT?

Look at the first part of the word, workout. It is work, it is supposed to be a challenge, and it does require some effort and energy. We in America are so used to comfort, ease and convenience that most people avoid any thing that makes them uncomfortable, tired, sweat or breathe hard. All of these things are actually good for us. If we stick with it long enough, in time we will see that these very things that make us uncomfortable do lead to improvements.

With initial exercise, soreness will probably occur after the first couple of work-out sessions. The body is not used to those new demands being placed upon it. Your body is trying to stop you because it is being made uncomfortable, but KEEP IT UP! The soreness is actually the first sign of progress. If you stop and sit out for weeks at a time and then attempt to work out again, you will get sore....again. The solution? Don't allow yourself to go days at a time without getting some type of exercise, stick with it.

When developing a physical activity program for life it is important to include: Strength or resistance training, cardiovascular activity, flexibility and balance training. All of these components are important. When developed they help with the daily demands of life. They also provide a great preventative measure not only to numerous lifestyle diseases but also to the natural decline of many activities that come with aging.

Look at the many benefits Cardiovascular activity, often referred to as aerobic activity, has to offer.

- Feel energized for hours afterwards
- It burns calories to help manage a healthy weight
- Strengthens the heart and lungs
- Alleviates depression (Interconnection—Helps emotional wellness)
- Improves short term memory (Interconnection—Helps mental wellness)
- Helps control diabetes, by acting as insulin
- Reduces resting and working heart rates
- Helps reduce the bad cholesterol (LDL) and raise the good (HDL)
- Improves endurance and stamina
- Helps with sleep disturbances
- Good way to manage stress
- Can help reduce blood pressure
- Provides time to plan and problem solve
- Reduces the risk of: colon, prostate and breast cancer
- Provides an opportunity to catch up on your reading by listening to an audio book.
- Exercising outside can help boost your Vitamin D intake
- Strengthens the immune system
- Increases bone density
- Improves circulation
- Live longer
- Helps manage a healthy weight

To be effective and reap the benefits above it is important to remember this acrostic F I T. **F**—Frequency, **I**—Intensity **T**—Time.

Frequency—Cardiovascular activity can be performed most days of the week. That means about four to six times each week. It is important to take at least one day off every week. Sometimes two might be necessary. If you have a week where you are forced to take three or four days off, don't get discouraged and think, *what's the use?* Just do what you can and then get back into your routine as soon as you can.

It is very important to make sure that your workouts are frequent enough. We human beings eat on a regular basis, so it is important to move our bodies on a regular basis. For you weekend warriors out there, Saturdays aren't enough!

Intensity—Your cardiovascular/aerobic activities need to be difficult enough to make you breathe hard and break a sweat. This doesn't mean you have to be doubled over gasping to take a breath. It just means your heart rate should rise because it is working harder to pump blood to your working muscles. When engaged in cardiovascular activity your effort level should be around a 6-8, on a scale of 1-10. A 1 would be the equivalent of sitting around watching television, a 10 would be an all-out effort requiring you to give your maximal effort. A simple way to determine if your cardiovascular activity is at the right intensity is to do a simple talk test. While exercising you should be able to answer questions and have a light conversation, but you should not be able to sing a song. So if you can belt out the Star Spangled Banner while you are walking, jogging or bicycling you need to take your intensity level up a notch or two.

Most people exercise at an easy comfortable 3-4 level. They can say they are exercising, but the fact is they don't want to be uncomfortable, so they don't exert themselves enough. This level of exercise is better than sitting at home finishing off a dozen donuts, but it is not intense enough to produce noticeable benefits.

This scale used when exercising is a personal evaluation. To one person jogging an eight minute mile might seem effortless however, to someone else; walking that same mile in 15 minutes may present a difficult struggle. The number you rank your effort at is not static, in time it will change and you will discover that the activities that once ranked as a 9 or 10 will be ranked at a 5 or 6.

Time—If you are not getting any type of cardiovascular activity right now, it is fine to start with five to ten minutes if necessary and then add two to four minutes every other day. Don't get frustrated and give up. If you do five minutes today, that is five minutes more than you did yesterday. You can also log several five to ten minute sessions together to give you a total of 30-40 minutes for the day. If you can go for a total of 30 minutes on your first work out …go for it. Just make sure you have the proper shoes and access to water for adequate hydration.

While working to reach your goal of 30-40 minutes of cardiovascular activity each day, you might get bored or start feeling a bit of fatigue. If this happens, try to mix-up the workout with intervals.

An interval is a term that simply means going hard or fast and then slowing down a bit, then going hard again. You can do intervals in a ratio of 30 sec. hard, then one to two minutes easy. In time you can make the hard section last as long or longer than the easy/recovery session. It is important to warm-up for five to ten minutes before you begin to increase the intensity of your workout.

You can also switch activities. If the walk around the neighborhood is boring you out of your mind switch it up with a bike ride or rent an exercise DVD, try out a local gym, jump rope, combine some jogging with walking. Listen to music. Praise and worship music is very inspiring and energizing, it helps direct your mind to God, which helps your spiritual development while you are pursuing physical wellness. Another option is, recruiting someone to exercise with you. This is a great way to help you get through a workout and also lends to the development of social wellness for the both of you.

Interconnection—Physical, Spiritual and Social

Weight training is a useful tool for weight loss & weight management.

Women are especially guilty of skipping weight training. Many women wrongly believe that weights will make them bulky, and many men have wrongly told women they need to go light and do a higher number of repetitions. Women listen up. This is not true! In order for women to build lean muscle mass, a load heavy enough to stress the muscles and stimulate muscle growth is required. The heavier weights will not make you look like a man. You don't have the testosterone that men have and women do not have as many muscle fibers as men do. Women are cursed with a higher number of fat cells. When I get to heaven I plan on asking God why he was so generous with the fat cells he gave us women. I personally am still struggling with being thankful for them.

A personal training client of mine had been diagnosed with multiple sclerosis 12 years prior to our meeting. This client had tried all types of treatments, remedies and alternative medications for her M.S. She even tried daily bee stings. She had also been on steroids and tried two different prescriptions. She got her physicians approval and came to me seeking assistance with weight loss and strength and flexibility training. After four months of training this client went back to her doctor for her annual physical. He told her that getting active and incorporating weight training into her routine was the most beneficial thing she had done for her M.S. symptoms and her overall health. Her strength, endurance and balance were all improved and her body fat was reduced. These physical improvements greatly improved her emotional and social health as well.

Check out the benefits weight training offers:

* Improves strength and balance by helping the joints and muscles work together more efficiently.

* Helps maintain strength and lean mass in cancer patients undergoing chemotherapy.

* Improves mobility in Parkinson's and multiple sclerosis patients.

* Helps reduce pain and stiffness to increase mobility in osteoarthritis, rheumatoid arthritis and fibromyalgia patients.

* Enhances immune function.

* Increases functionality in the areas of: flexibility, mobility, balance and stamina.

* Helps with weight loss because muscle is hungry. It takes more calories to sustain muscle than to sustain fat. Fat seems to stay whether we feed it or not.

* True strength training can burn more calories than some cardiovascular activities.

* Obese individuals can find some vigorous exercise to be uncomfortable. Working with free weights or strength training machines is frequently more enjoyable to them.

* Weight training also called resistance training, helps increase bone density.

* Helps reduce muscular imbalances thereby reducing the risk of some type of injuries.

* Helps with maintenance of functionality into older age.

* Improves sleep patterns.

* Has been shown to help reduce blood pressure.

The average person doesn't have a strong desire to look like the body builders we see on those television competitions. These competitors spend hours every day in the gym and they also use products to stimulate muscle growth. The weight training necessary to promote good physical health takes only 30 minutes per day or an hour every other day. This depends on how you divide the muscle groups to be worked.

Weight training can be done before or after a cardio work-out. Recent studies have shown that more calories are burned when

weights are done before cardio. The main thing to remember is ….
JUST DO IT!

Sometimes life takes over and a walk has to be done early in the morning and weights are done after work. On those days where everything is going well and your schedule isn't triple booked you might be able to get your cardio and weight training done in one setting and be done for the day. Sometimes weight training can be done first thing in the morning but cardio has to be done at the soccer or baseball field while the kids are practicing.

When doing weight training it is important to give each muscle group a day off after lifting. This is important because when effective weight training is done, tiny little tears occur in the muscles (micro-traumas) these tears are necessary for muscle and strength gains, but adequate rest must be given to them. Some people find that they prefer to lift weights every day, but these people work different muscle groups each day. Others find it more convenient to lift weights every other day and work all nine major muscle groups at each training session. I underscored major because there are numerous other muscles on your body, but the major ones are important for basic physical wellness.

These nine muscle groups are:

1. Gluteus Maximus (Butt)
2. Quadriceps (Thigh)
3. Hamstrings (Back of leg)
4. Pectorals (Chest)
5. Deltoids (Shoulders)
6. Triceps (Back of arms)
7. Biceps (Front of arms)
8. Latissimus dorsi, Trapezius & Rhomboids (Back)
9. Rectus abdominis, external & internal obliques and transverse abdominal (Abdominals)

All nine major muscle groups need to be worked two to three times per week. Various strength training programs are available in magazines, books or on the internet. Look for one that promotes total wellness, not just a body weight or bulk.

Do keep in mind that muscle is denser than fat, but it is healthier and more beneficial to you. So when you start your weight training program it would be a good idea for you to take your measurements, your weight and if possible find out what your body fat percentage is and write it down. Body fat percentage is the percentage of body fat you have compared to the percentage of lean muscle mass. This is not BMI (Body Mass Index) which is calculated by a person's height and weight. It is good to know both numbers.

Before moving on to flexibility training, I have a reminder for you. In order for any physical activity to be effective it must be done on a regular basis, intensely enough over an extended period of time.... Like the rest of your life!

<u>Flexibility training (stretching)</u>

Flexibility—A joint's ability to move through a full range of motion. Flexibility training or stretching is helpful not only for flexibility but also for strengthening. This type of activity can also be a way to get a sedentary person to move and become friends with their body, or like my sister, who said "I don't like to sweat." She started attending a class for stretching, stress reduction and relaxation purposes, and after a few years she has advanced to a boot-camp type class that meets each morning at 5:00 a.m.

The flexibility training class opened a door to physical activity for her and let her see that all physical activity is not uncomfortable or strenuous. Now physical activity is part of her normal routine.

Group fitness classes are great and I would encourage everyone to give them a try. They however are not mandatory to improve flexibility. This is something that can be done on your own.

Many people skip stretching because it seems there are no physical benefits. Stretching doesn't build muscle, burn many calories or improve your endurance. Flexibility training however, does offer the following benefits:

* Increased physical performance—A flexible joint has the ability to move through a greater range of motion and requires less energy to do so.

* Reduced muscle soreness—Recent studies show that slow static stretching done **after** exercising helps reduce muscle soreness. Static—slow, gradual and controlled elongation of a muscle. Stretch is held for 15-30 seconds with a pulling sensation, but no pain.

* Improved posture and balance—Many people's soft tissue structures have adopted poorly to the effects of gravity and poor postural habits. Stretching can realign soft tissue structures, thus reducing the effort it takes to maintain good posture.

* Increases synovial fluid which is a lubricating fluid.

* Increases blood and nutrients to tissue—Tissue temperature raises which improves circulation and nutrient transport.

* Improved muscle coordination—Nerve impulse and velocity is increased.

* Helps relax the mind and body after exercising.

* Decreases risk of injury—Resistance in tissue structures is decreased by stretching. This reduces your chance of injury due to exceeding tissue extensibility during activity.

Flexibility training doesn't have to be complicated and it takes only five to ten minutes. Stretch your hamstrings, quadriceps, calves, triceps, chest and back. Individuals who run need to take time to specifically stretch their Achilles tendons and calf muscles to avoid plantar fasciitis. The hamstrings, hip flexors and quadriceps also need stretching to help with efficient stride.

Years ago and still today many still feel they must stretch before exercising. This is fine because it helps eliminate stiffness and increases blood flow. But, since it is done while the muscle is a cold, it results in what is called an elastic stretch. Which means that it stretches out but goes right back, just like elastic. It is more beneficial to stretch after exercising. A muscle is warmed through exercising, and when it is stretched it is less likely to be injured and it also makes a permanent increase in flexibility. This type of stretch is called a plastic stretch. Think of it like this. You have a drinking straw or other piece of plastic that has been heated over a flame and then stretch it out. You will see that it stays in the stretched position, it does not bounce back.

Chapter 13

REPLENISH, REST AND RENEW

So now we know how important physical activity is and we are all going to start today...right? Just as important as working out, so too is the rest and recovery process. If God rested on the seventh day after creating earth and man, it might be wise for us to follow his example. A healthy eating plan and physical activity are only parts of the formula necessary to develop physical wellness. Just as important is healthy replenishment and adequate sleep.

When considering the re-fueling of your body, it is most beneficial to eat within 1 hour of working out, if possible. This is when your body is most receptive to re-fueling. This snack or meal should contain some protein for tissue repair and carbohydrates to replenish your glycogen levels. This can be something as simple as a peanut butter sandwich with a sliced banana on whole wheat bread and a glass of skim milk, or a turkey sandwich, or a bowl of whole grain cereal with sliced almonds or walnuts. There are a few good protein and meal replacement bars on the market. Use these bars only on occasion, and be sure to read the labels and check for high levels of sugar and fat. When possible choose whole food it is best for you.

Be sure to include plenty of water throughout the day, not only after working out. Since water makes up approximately 60% of our body, and 85% of our brain, it is very important. Water is the ideal diet drink, no calories, sodium, sugar, fat, artificial sweeteners, preservatives or coloring. The benefits of water include:

- Natural appetite suppression; many people eat when they actually are thirsty.

- Helps with fluid retention by reducing sodium build up.
- Assists the body in the metabolism of fat.
- Helps eliminate toxins from the body.
- Helps maintain muscle tone.
- Help keeps the body cool.
- Helps with regularity.

<u>Go to bed already!</u>

Erroneously, many people think that staying up late burns calories. Not so, because sleep provides time for our bodies to heal and restore themselves. A good work-out routine is only really good if there is adequate recovery. The process of getting physically strong and healthy is actually a process of tearing down and then building up. Keep in mind, if you keep tearing down you won't get the results you want and worse yet you could get a serious injury or illness due to over training. In addition to sleeping seven to eight hours nightly, adequate recovery also includes taking at least one day off from exercising each week.

Everyone has a sleepless night from time to time, but research shows that lack of sleep on a regular basis can cause numerous problems. Weight gain is common. This is because a lack of sleep causes our bodies to revert to survival mechanism and the metabolism slows down. A study done on 35,000 Japanese workers at an electric power company showed that those who got six hours or less of sleep per night were twice as likely to gain weight as those who routinely got seven to eight hours each night.

Those who consistently lack sleep (six or less hours per night) have a greater chance of developing or dying from heart disease, and a 15 percent greater chance of developing or dying from a stroke, become less sensitive to insulin, have blurred vision, irritability, inability to concentrate, fatigue, memory lapses and bags and/or dark circles under the eyes.

Obvious tips for sleep problems

—Avoid all caffeine after 12:00 noon. This means: tea, soda, energy drinks and chocolate, not just coffee.

—Avoid late or long naps. If you feel dead tired after you get home from work or school, get up and go outside, go for a walk or drink a glass of cool water. Then go to bed a bit earlier if needed.

—Establish a bedtime routine. Our mothers knew what they were doing when they put us to bed and had the lights out by 9:00. We need to follow this wisdom. Go to bed and wake up at the same time every day. If followed long enough it will become something you body adapts to and sleep will come. God made our bodies able to adapt, it is up to us to provide the right things for them to adapt to.

—Quiet your mind. Another thing our mothers taught us was to say our prayers before going to bed. The best way to end my day is to pray and talk to my Heavenly Father. When was the last time you talked to Father? He wants to hear from you too!

—Relax. Avoid engaging in stressful or strenuous activities, or heated discussions for at least two to three hours before your planned bed time. Also try reading a book, one by Shakespeare or one of my kid's European history books always puts me to sleep.

Some not so obvious tips

—Turn all the lights and television off. Try to make your sleeping area as dark as possible. Your brain produces melatonin to help you sleep, but it only produces it when it is dark.

—Keep some paper and a pen by your bed. Write down things that need to be done tomorrow, or things that are bugging you. That way you don't worry about forgetting to take care of them. They can wait until the morning. Everyone else is sleeping anyway so not much business or work matters can be taken care of at 2:00 a.m.

—Some cold medicines that have warnings of causing drowsiness can actually have the opposite effect on many people and keep them awake.

—Diet pills may not contain caffeine, but if they promise energy, check out the ingredients. There is probably a stimulant in the diet pill that may interfere with sleep.

—Don't get worked up and worried about not being able to sleep. It happens to everyone on occasion. Sometimes our own anxiety about not sleeping interferes with our nodding off.

—As difficult as it sounds, don't sleep in if you had trouble going to sleep or woke-up several times. Make yourself get up and go through the day as usual. Your chances of going to sleep the next night will be better.

—God made our bodies extremely intelligent and readily adaptable. They know what they need. If you go without sleep long enough, your body will usually take over in time and eventually you will sleep. If not get it checked out.

In conclusion of the discussion on Physical wellness, I once more want to point out the importance of developing and adhering to a healthy lifestyle. Keep in mind that your choices do matter and they are very powerful, you will be left to live with the consequences of your choices, good or bad. If you can't find the motivation to take care of yourself for you, do it for those who love you.

Do it so that you are more equipped to complete the physically demanding tasks that ministry can require. Take care of you because God loves you and He gave His son for you. You are immensely valuable and God has a specific purpose for your life. Don't let physical limitations, weakness or lack of energy stop you from enjoying the life that Jesus came to give.

Chapter 14

MENTAL & EMOTIONAL WELLNESS, ACCENTUATE THE POSITIVE

Our mind is the most powerful tool we possess. Everything we do, say or think originates from a thought. It might be a conscious thought that we are vividly aware of or it might be a thought we are not even slightly aware of. Think about this. Have you ever had someone come up and ask what you were thinking? Your response was…. "nothing", and you really meant it, you weren't trying to be evasive or dishonest. You really didn't think you were thinking about anything specifically. We are always thinking, it's something we do without even trying. At times however, it may appear that we didn't think at all, based on our words or choices. Our minds never stop, but our minds often stop us.

When most people speak of mental or emotional wellness they are usually speaking of the same thing. The terms are frequently interchanged and one is dependent on the other. This is why I am covering them together. They however are not the same.

Mental is referring to our thoughts and numerous other cognitive processes of the mind. Sometimes thoughts are good, based in truth and rational; sometimes they are irrational and delusional because they are based in untruths.

Emotional usually refers to the feelings our thoughts evoke. The word emotion comes from the combining the two Latin words E, which means out of, and the word movere' which means move. Hence we get, that which results from, or our English word emotion. Motivation is also derived from this same word.

Thoughts frequently lead to emotions, but emotions always result from thoughts. Our emotions do not come from the actions of others, circumstances or problems. Our emotions come from our thoughts or perceptions about these things. Our thoughts, although they are unseen, are very powerful. They are the catalyst to our every word, action or feeling. The way we think can literally change our lives.

Consider this scenario; a busy woman gets stuck at work and ends up having to stay an extra two hours at the office. She doesn't make it home in time to have dinner ready for her spouse. Husband #1 is angry because he thinks of this as inconsideration on her part and feels she doesn't value him. He assumes that she knows that her having dinner ready when he gets home is very important to him. Same scenario, but with couple #2 the husband discovers his wife is not home and starts fixing dinner, he feels concerned for her because he thinks she will be tired and feel rushed because she got stuck at work late. Different thoughts lead to different emotions which lead to different actions.

Thoughts → Emotions/Beliefs → Behavior

Our minds are a very powerful muscle. I know the mind isn't really a muscle, but it does function much like a muscle in that it is powerful, it can do great works, and it can be strengthened like a muscle. Likewise, the unused mind can become weak. The mind leads us, helps store information, solve problems, and it also manufactures the thoughts that evoke our emotions, which generate a response or action or in some cases a refusal to respond or act.

Why are our thoughts so powerful? Mainly, because of the emotions and beliefs they cause. Emotions are not inherently good or bad, they are normal human responses. The word of God even tells us "Be angry and sin not" (Ephesians 4:6). The problems come when our thoughts are based on untruths and things that are not in-line with the word of God. These thoughts produce some type of emotion. If the thoughts are in-line with the word of God and we believe them, we are more likely to respond or take actions that result in good. However, if our thoughts are selfish, hurtful, critical, lustful, resentful, envious, or based on lies of Satan, they cause emotions that can lead us to engage in unhealthy or self-defeating behaviors that not only hurt ourselves but have the potential to hurt others as well.

A modern day example of passion is played out in two different scenarios. A passion that is motivated by a desire to obey God's word to feed the hungry and defend the weak, leads an individual or group to develop a ministry that helps alleviate one of the many forms of human suffering. This is wonderful. Passion however, based on selfish or ungodly agendas can prompt the development of some very ungodly developments. An example is the pro-choice movement which favors the killing of unborn children. Another example is the founding of the LGBT organization. This is a group that supports the lesbian, gay, bisexual and transgender lifestyles. All passion was not created equal. As Larry Winget says in his book, *It's Called Work for a Reason,* "People can be passionately wrong." The latter two groups are an example of this.

Unfortunately, we are living in a time in which lies and deceit abound. The father of lies never rests. His lies are feeding thoughts that are leading to strong emotions which are resulting in terrible choices and behaviors. Numerous religions and cultures have lived and died according to belief systems and emotions built upon lies.

We Christians are not immune from building our thoughts and belief systems on untruths. These untruths cause us to have thoughts that produce: doubt, anger, hopelessness, shame and fear. One of the most effective ways that Satan tries to defeat Christians in their personal walk with Jesus is to make them doubt what God says is true. Look back in Genesis to how he convinced Eve to disobey God, by causing her to doubt God's goodness.

Satan knows he has been defeated and he knows he can't get our soul if we have received Jesus into our lives. However, he is happy to get into our minds and convince us of his destructive lies. The lies of the devil are effective because they are very well disguised and believable. They can rob us of joy and victory, and prevent us from enjoying the abundance that Jesus came to give. Perceptions and personal belief systems built upon un–Godly, untruths are very damaging. Why? Because belief predicts behavior.

What is this thing called mental wellness?

Most people think of and describe mental wellness as, the absence of a major mental health condition, this is similar to the definition of physical wellness; the absence of illness or disease. These two definitions originate from an avoidance mind-set. Yes, we should avoid harmful behaviors, God gave us brains for a reason and we should use them. However fear should not dominate us or prevent us from pursuing and enjoying the beautiful gifts that God provides.

When we make the decision to work towards healthy thinking that lines up with the word of God, we are taking steps that can lead to emotional peace and stability. Working towards something is being proactive, and it means we are pursuing something good rather than fearing or avoiding something bad.

Being proactive can be very energizing to us, it can also be an invitation or encouragement to others to do the same.

The difference in the avoidance of mental illness vs. the pursuit of mental wellness is that, when we strive towards mental or physical wellness, we are considering those two components as good, valuable and desirable assets. They are things people aspire to. This process of aspiring to or working towards something can help us focus on the positive. Focusing on the positive can actually increase feelings of wellbeing. These feelings can help motivate and energize us, which is helpful in everything we do.

On the other hand, attempts at trying to stop our negative, critical or unhealthy thinking, present a difficult challenge. Constant avoidance and attempts at the elimination of negative behavior or thinking requires a great amount of will power which can lead to a feeling of self deprivation. This robs energy, and frequently, while in the process of trying to stop stinking thinking, people often condemn themselves, get frustrated or angry at themselves or go engage in some type of (usually unbeneficial) distraction. This attempt to stop stinking thinking is much like the swearing off of a certain food. Once we say that we are no longer eating a particular food. What happens? That food is everywhere, and when it isn't visions and thoughts of that food fill our mind. Sometimes we even hear that chocolate brownie or extra cheese pizza all the way in the kitchen calling us by name!

Since being proactive is good, what do we strive for ?

Let's look below at a few definitions of mental wellness:

1. A state of emotional well-being in which an individual is able to use his or her cognitive and emotional capabilities to function in society, meet the demands of everyday life and cope with and adjust to the stresses of life in an acceptable and healthy way.

2. The World Health Organization defines mental health as: a state of well-being in which the individual realizes his or her own abilities, can cope with the normal stresses of life, can work productively and fruitfully, and is able to make a contribution to his or her community.

Based on both of these definitions we realize that, mental wellness is something we all need and desire. It expresses the ability to function independently and deal with life in a healthy and productive manner. There are however, some days we all question our mental functioning.... or lack thereof.

3. The best definition of mental wellness, like the definition of wholeness is found in the Bible. Mental wellness—Having the

mind of Christ. Philippians 2:5 implores us, "Let this mind be in you which was also in Christ Jesus." Jesus displayed perfection in every thought, emotion and choice of His life.

Since mental wellness is best described as having the mind of Christ, it is only fitting that the Bible is the handbook. We can know that it has the answers to help us with our thinking, which by-the-way will help us with everything, all temptations included. God created our mind, and its many fascinating processes, knowing this, we should seek our Creator to discover and follow His ways.

As human beings we do three things, we think, we feel, we do. Those three things may at times, not appear to be in that order because often an unwise word is spoken or a foolish choice is made that causes a little introspection on our part. We then think that what we felt caused us to react, or not. The feeling did motivate us to act, but that feeling was birthed through a thought. We have all made statements we felt foolish about and claimed later that, *we just weren't thinking.* We were thinking all right, it just wasn't a very intelligent thought. If we change our thinking our feelings and actions will follow.

Our thoughts and beliefs are so important that numerous pastors, professors, psychologist and leadership experts base a majority of their teaching on the thought process and our mind-set. John Maxwell in his book, *How Successful People Think* said, "I've studied successful people for forty years, and though the diversity you find among them is astounding, I believe they are all alike in one way: how they think! That is the one thing that separates the successful from the unsuccessful. The good news is that it's possible to learn how to think like a successful person."

God the greatest author of all-time, knew that our thoughts could help us achieve success, and He also knew our thoughts could cause many problems. Ezekiel 38:10 relates, "On that day it shall come to pass that thoughts will arise in your mind, and you will make an evil plan." Where do evil plans come from? Thoughts that arise in our minds.

Brian Tracy: CEO, motivational speaker and author of 45 books summed it up nicely in the title of one of his books, *Change Your Thinking, Change Your Life.* I wonder if Mr. Tracy got the title of that book from Romans 12:2, "And do not be conformed to this world, but be transformed by the renewing of your mind, that you may prove what is that good and acceptable and perfect will of God." To be transformed is to be changed. This verse clearly tells us that we are changed by the renewing of our minds.

The key here is, the working of the Holy Spirit to renew our minds and then transform (change) us. The Holy Spirit changes our thinking through our consistent study and meditation on the Scriptures.

Begin with the beginning

Changing our thinking requires us to take personal inventory of our thoughts. It means being aware of our thoughts and then checking to see if they line up with the truths of God. This process takes mindfulness, diligence and brutal honesty. It is a difficult process because our thoughts and perceptions start being programmed in us the day we come into this world. Negative, critical, or fearful thinking can become a habit, and we aren't even aware that we are doing it.

Our current mind-set is largely the result of seeing how our parents and others around us responded and dealt with everyday life. It can be very difficult to realize that the teachings and values we grew up with, believed in and built our lives on may not be based in God's truth, it shakes our foundation. Regardless of what church we grew up in, what our grandparents taught us, or what religion our parents were, our knowledge of God's truth is now our responsibility. He will reveal His truth to us if we seek Him. Our Father wants us to know and live in His truths.

Once we begin this personal inventory, and become aware of thoughts that run contrary to the word of God, we need to follow the instructions found in 2 Corinthians 10:5, "Casting down arguments and every high thing that exalts itself against the knowledge of God, bringing every thought into captivity to the obedience of Christ."

In order to do this we must know what things exalt themselves against the knowledge of God. This begins with a daily time of reading and memorizing the scriptures. We provide nourishment to our physical bodies every day. We should make it a priority to nourish our minds and spirits with the Word of Truth everyday.

Once we cast down these arguments we need to make sure that we have Godly food prepared to replace them. What do we feed our minds? Philippians 4:8 says, "Finally, brethren, whatever things are true, whatever things are noble, whatever things are just, whatever things are pure, whatever things are lovely, whatever things are of good report, if there is any virtue and if there is anything praiseworthy—meditate on these things"

In order to "think on these things", two actions are required of us. First, we need to learn what "these things" are. Then we need to meditate on them. All of us learn better when more than one of our senses is engaged in the learning process. When we begin scripture memorization we can increase our learning by engaging a few of our senses in the following way:

First: For visual learning, engage your eyes and mind by reading the Bible. Find and study the many promises and commands that God makes.

Next: For auditory learning, engage your ears by reading them out loud.

Last: For kinesthetic learning; engage your hands and write the verses down. When we learn scripture we are building the foundation for wholeness. God's word is the believer's ammunition for the lies and temptations that Satan throws at us. "Your word I have hidden in my heart, That I might not sin against You" (Psalm 119:11).

Once we have read, written and memorized the scriptures, we then have to consciously choose to believe them. This can be difficult at times. It is hard to believe that God shall supply all our needs when we've been unemployed for 18 months and the bank just sent a foreclosure notice on our home. It's hard to believe that all things will workout for good when you have been diagnosed with terminal cancer and you have no health insurance.

Confess your doubts to God, ask Him to help you believe. You are not on your own through any of your journeys. We are reminded of this in Psalms 46:1, "God is our refuge and strength, A very present help in time of trouble." When doubts come, and they will, draw from the scripture bank in your mind and repeat the truths and promises of God out loud. Repeat it again and again if necessary. We are more likely to believe what we tell ourselves rather than what someone else tells us.

His word is written for our benefit. His truths will help our mental wellness when we intentionally use them to replace thinking that doesn't line up with His word. This intentionality of choosing our thoughts in the manner that God states is imperative. The Bible is the ultimate reference for dealing with unhealthy thoughts and emotions. "You will keep him in perfect peace, whose mind is stayed on You, Because he trusts in You" (Isaiah 26:3).

Some components of a healthy mind

Dr. Ron Sterling; a general and Geriatric Psychiatrist, and author of numerous books on mental wellness developed a list of five factors of mental wellness. Although Dr. Sterling makes no reference to Scripture, it is interesting that the factors he listed can be found in some Biblical principles. I have added the Biblical perspective on some of them.

1. Self appreciation - We can all point out our flaws and weakness pretty easily, but we need to also be able to notice what is right with us

and appreciate our strengths. Since God, the creator of the entire universe loves and sent His Son to die for us we should learn to love ourselves, not because we are good and not out of arrogance but because, when we accept Jesus as our Savior the Bible says, "For He made Him who knew no sin to be sin for us, that we might become the righteousness of God in Him" (II Corinthians 5:21). He is our sufficiency, strength, salvation, peace, hope, love, provider, shield and He is enough.

If the weakening thoughts of: shame, condemnation, fear or self-criticalness start calling to you, take comfort in the verse above and also remember Philippians 1:6, "Be confident of this very thing, that He who has begun a good work in you will complete it until the day of Jesus Christ." We are all works in progress, and His grace is sufficient!

Interconnection—Mental and emotional wellness will be developed when pursuing Spiritual wellness.

2. Resilience - This is the ability to deal with and recover from hardship, misfortune, change and shock. The qualities that foster resilience are:

—Optimism (hope) "Now hope does not disappoint, because the love of God has been poured out in our hearts by the Holy Spirit who was given to us" (Romans 5:5).

—A sense of perspective (seeing the big picture), believing that there is a positive meaning to life. "For I know the plans that I have for you, declares the Lord. Plans to prosper you and not harm you, plans to give you a hope and a future" (Jeremiah 29:11 NIV).

—The ability to laugh at some at some of the tricks that life plays on us. Life is hard; we may as well get used to it and come to expect it. God tells us so in his word. "These things I have spoken to you, that in Me you may have peace. In this world you will have tribulation; but be of good cheer, I have overcome the world" (John 16:33). Memorize this verse and lean on it when circumstances seem unbearable.

3. Inclusion - The ability to allow ourselves to get close to others. We all need to develop give-and-take relationships and mutually supportive social networks. This development leads to the realization that life is not all about us. As Christians we are part of the family of God, there is power and strength in this family. Christians need the support and encouragement of other followers who are working to build the Kingdom of God. Proverbs 26:4 says, "And in the multitude of counselors there is safety."

More verses confirming the need for others is found in Hebrews 10:24-25, "And let us consider one another in order to stir up love and good works, not forsaking the assembling of ourselves together as is the manner of some but exhorting one another, and so much the more as you see the Day approaching."

Interconnection—Inclusion is not just helpful for our mental and emotional wellness it also helps in our social wellness, which can help our mental and emotional wellness. Our mental and emotional wellness however helps with our inclusion. This is a case of which came first, the chicken or the egg? Our mental, emotional and social wellness are helpful to each other while at the same time dependent upon each other.

4. Negotiation - The ability to see that we may not have all the answers and then allow ourselves to learn from others, and if necessary, the ability to alter our beliefs when new data or information is presented. It is imperative to know that the word of God is the ultimate rule and it is 100 percent truth, 100 percent of the time. Others may have opinions and beliefs but if they are contrary to what God says we are to reject them. That being stated, it is also necessary to realize from time to time we might be wrong. Yes, even Christians have disagreements.... shocking I know. But, mental wellness demonstrates an ability to negotiate and handle conflicts in a manner that is pleasing and acceptable to God. Keep in mind this might not always be pleasing to people. The ability to negotiate includes the ability to use logic and focus on facts not

emotions, the ability to communicate and problem solve, and it also reflects the ability to control our emotions and mouth.

<u>5. Exercise, curiosity and leisure activities</u> - These are tools that have consistently shown to enhance mental wellness. Research shows that physical exercise helps with depression, playing board games or musical instruments, dancing and reading all help enhance brain functioning and reduce the risk of dementia. Laughter and having fun fall into this category. Remember the phrase "laughter is good medicine."

<u>Interconnection</u>—Mental wellness cannot be separated from physical, social and spiritual wellness.

Four of the five qualities mentioned above are mostly non-visible occurrences, thoughts, perceptions or beliefs that lead to feelings which can lead to actions or a refusal to act. The fifth one, exercise, curiosity and leisure activities are mostly actions or physical responses however, where do you think all of these actions and physical responses originate?

<u>Control your emotions so they don't control you</u>

Our society tends to express emotions as a negative thing. People often say, "don't get so emotional" but, emotions get people going. They can fuel a dream or desire for years. However, it is good to keep this little phrase in mind. "Emotions motivate but facts need to dictate." God's word is fact. It might not make sense to us, and his word sometimes blows our feeble minds…but it is fact! Mental wellness grows and develops from learning and believing the truth of God, and living and making decisions in line with His word.

In a short re-cap I am repeating: We think, we feel, we do. Emotions in and of themselves aren't bad or good. What does the Bible say about emotions? Quite a bit, but the word emotions or emotional is never used in the Bible. There are many types of emotions mentioned. Anger is mentioned 270 times, Joy-242, grief -35, mourning-47, mourn-138, terror-88, Sadness/sorrow 1, frightened- 9.

Emotions are not bad and they are not a display of weakness. David, the giant-slayer, frequently expressed emotions, just check out Psalm. David was a man after God's own heart and he voices a full range of emotions which include: desperation, sorrow, anger, fear, vengeance, praise, peace, thankfulness and joy.

Jesus experienced emotions including: delight, grief, anguish, He sympathizes with our weakness and He was in all points tempted, yet without sin. Jesus experienced being troubled, deeply distressed, and exceedingly sorrowful, even to death. God experiences emotions and they range from anger found in Exodus 4:14, "So the anger of the Lord was kindled against Moses." To pleasure, 1 Chronicles 29:17, "I know also, my God, that you test the heart and have pleasure in uprightness." He continually displays the greatest emotion, love. "For God so loved the world that He gave His only begotten son, that who so ever believeth in Him shall not perish but have ever lasting life" (John 3:16).

The problem doesn't lie within our human emotions, but rather in the fact that we too often allow them to dictate our behavior rather than the truths of the Bible. We are warned about this in Jeremiah 17:9, "The heart is deceitful above all things, and desperately wicked; who can know it?" As Christians all our behaviors should be dictated by the truths found in the Bible, not our fickle moods or circumstances. The more we focus on and trust in the truths of the Bible the less likely we are to be deceived and led by our emotions.

There is help for our emotions

God does care about our emotions. Psalm 34:18 reminds us, "The Lord is near to those who have a broken heart, and saves those who have a contrite spirit." Another verse letting us know that God cares about our emotions is found in Isaiah 61:1, "The Spirit of the Lord is upon me, because the Lord has anointed me to preach good tidings to the poor; He has sent me to heal the broken hearted, to proclaim liberty to the captives and the opening of the prison to those who are bound." There are two things I would like to point out in this verse. First, if the Lord anoints someone to heal the broken hearted it obviously means it is important to Him. Second, all prisons aren't made with concrete blocks and metal bars, there are many hurting people in our world today living in invisible prisons.

These invisible prisons can come in many forms, they can show up as: addictions, obsessions, fear, depression, denial, deception through secular teaching, eating disorders, betrayal, loneliness, anger, anxiety, self-hatred, bitterness, unforgiveness, criticalness and the list could go on. The point is that our hearts, minds and spirits are typically the source of our battles. When we face defeat or damage in one of these unseen areas it is often manifested in our physical health, social health, financial health or spiritual health.

Both mental and emotional illnesses are hard to measure, but they can be improved in everyone. Psychologists and counselors state that no one is perfectly mentally well, and that no one is completely mentally ill. Personally I have been around a few people that make me want to challenge the last part of that statement.

Deliberately choose what you allow to occupy your mind

Our reading and taking in of God's word is the best thing we can do for our wholeness, in fact it is essential. God never changes, He never lies and you can trust Him. You can and you must choose your thoughts, which will help you trust Him. It might be difficult, nevertheless.... God has equipped you to do this! II Timothy 1:7 tells us, "But God has not given us the spirit of fear, but of power and of love and of a sound mind." God has given you a sound mind. Now it is up to you to believe this promise, receive it and walk in it.

Proverbs 3:5-6 admonishes, "Trust in the Lord with all your heart: and lean not unto thine own understandings. In all thy ways acknowledge him and he shall direct thy paths."

*Mental illness should never be minimized. It is a very real struggle and it can be disabling. It can present itself in numerous manners and ranges from being severe in some to very slight in others. We should never shame or condemn someone who is dealing with any type of mental illness. It is a very common struggle; in fact all of us have some level of distorted thinking. This means we all need help at some point in our lives. Some individuals may require a Doctor's care for any chemical imbalances.

Chapter 15

SOCIAL/RELATIONAL WELLNESS

We all need others to some degree. Some people are extremely social, while others prefer quiet solitude, but people by nature are gregarious creatures. This means that people in general have a liking for companionship. They seek and enjoy the company of others. Gregariousness is actually a characteristic of living organisms.

Very early in history, God confirmed our needs for others in Genesis 2:18, "And the Lord God said, 'It is not good that a man should be alone,' I will make him a helper comparable to him." If God in His infinite wisdom knew that we needed help and even made a helper for us, what makes us think we know better than our Creator?

Our need for others is further confirmed in Ecclesiastes 4:8, "There is one alone, without companion: he has neither son nor brother. Yet there is no end to all his labors, nor is his eye satisfied with riches. But, he never asks, for whom do I toil and deprive myself of good? This also is vanity and a grave misfortune."

This fellow sounds sad and lonely. He works, but for what? Reading on from here to verses 9-12 we find a contrast. There is a listing of the benefits of companionship. "Two are better than one, because they have a good reward for their labor. For if they fall one will lift up his companion, but woe to him who is alone when he falls, for he has no one to help him up. Again, if two lie down together, they will keep warm; but how can one be warm alone? Though one may be overpowered by another, two can withstand him and a threefold cord is not quickly broken."

Look over those verses above once more. Each one of the benefits listed provides practical help for us in life, and they are available through others. When considering our social wellness we need to keep in mind that it is different from the components of physical, mental, spiritual and to a certain degree; financial wellness because, the determinants of social wellness exist outside of us. Our social wellness always involves others in some way. This is why it can be so frustrating at times.

Obstacles to social wellness

I am hesitant to offer this bit of self disclosure; but personally I feel that social wellness is the most difficult of all components of wholeness to develop, mostly because we are all imperfect and broken people. We are wounded warriors. The experiences of life have hurt us. Psalm 109:22 says, "For I am poor and needy, and my heart is wounded within me." Anyone living in this world, Christians included will experience failure, pain, rejection, fear or frustration, and we acquire scars from these experiences. However personal problems that we go through can actually provide a bridge that connects us with others who are dealing with the same struggles.

It is difficult in the face of painful and frightening struggles but, we can be comforted by reminding ourselves that these things are the very building blocks God uses to sanctify us and equip us to be His warriors. Without these unpleasant events in our lives we could not and would not have the opportunity to become strengthened and grow. Without trials we would never come to know that God can be our provider of all things. Trials are to our lives and character much like weights and other types of resistance are to our muscles; they grow and become strong and efficient for doing work, only after they have faced resistance, and moved through that resistance. No resistance = No strength.

Each of us is born with a unique personality, designed by God. This personal uniqueness, combined with the numerous and painful events in our lives, results in a great diversity of personalities, fears, desires and coping mechanisms. Social wellness requires that somehow, we are to develop and maintain peaceful and fulfilling relationships amidst all this diversity. The difficulty of maintaining peaceful and fulfilling relationships is compounded by the fact that none of us are completely mentally, physically, financially, emotionally, socially or spiritually well all of the time, so we are almost always carrying around some type of burden or longing that diverts our time, attention and energy. This heavy load can also bury our peace, compassion and generosity.

The combination of personal woundedness, unique personalities and various experiences is what presents one of the biggest challenges in the field of social services. A program that helps one person can be harmful to another. One person talks non-stop about themselves, while another will not offer any personal information. A goal that motivates one can completely deactivate another. One person finds sobriety at A. A. meetings, another finds the meetings depressing. There are adults who had a happy and safe childhood, while others feared going home each day. Some people like hot weather, some want it cold. There are generous souls around us, but there seems to be twice as many Scrooge-like ones. Some personalities are drawn to physical demands while others are energized by intellectual challenges. The list of diversities of personalities and struggles could take up pages....AND God knows about them all!

Diversity: God loves it, we fear it

God is a marvelously talented creator and He loves diversity and variety. Yet this causes many problems for us. What causes us so much trouble when dealing with people who are different? Part of this difficulty comes from our own selfishness.

We are told this in James 4:1-3, "Where do wars and fights come from among you? Do they not come from your desires for pleasure that war in your members? You lust and do not have. You murder and covet and cannot obtain. You fight and war. Yet you do not have because you do not ask. You ask and do not receive, because you ask amiss, that you may spend it on your pleasures."

The verses above clearly express a cause for social problems. We are selfish and think of our own personal desires and pleasures, we really only want to hear about things that interest us. We prefer to be around and associate with those who share our values, beliefs, political and religious views and hobbies because these people frequently have goals similar to ours.

The verses go on further to speak of our selfishness because too often when we see others succeed or amass great wealth through diligence and hard work, we don't celebrate or congratulate them, we covet. The last part of those verses say that we may pray, but our prayers aren't answered, because our requests are based on our own desire for personal pleasure. We take our eyes and minds off of Christ and His love for mankind and we set them on ourselves and our plans.

There are however, those occasions when a group of believers get together and are able to set goals that are mutually agreed upon, and the goals have the potential to benefit the entire group. Yet even when goals and objectives are agreed upon and set, another problem can result from resistance to, and fear of diversity. This is because each of us has a personal agenda in reaching this goal. We know what we want, and we believe we know the best way to get it. Our plans are structured and designed to meet our expectations. People who are different might get in the way of our plans.

When our plans are based solely on our own experience, knowledge and preferences they are less than optimal because we are relying only on what we know and what we have experienced. We forget that different people have different experiences, different desires and different talents; this is because God has a different call on their life. These differences can help strengthen the body of Christ.

The problem with rejecting those who are different here is two-fold: First, our selfishness and self-centeredness opposes compassion, generosity and a willingness to consider different ideas or people, which can hinder the reaching of a new or different group of people. Second, our sense of self-sufficiency, and refusal to accept, listen to or even consider people who are different from us can result in conflict or a weak and less than optimal solution. Neither of these displays social wellness.

In time, as we draw closer to our Father and become more Christ-like, we will begin to love others more, even those who are different than us. We will also become more focused on doing the will of our Father rather than our own. These developments will help strengthen our concern for the desires and needs of others. This is a real life example of unity in action (Chapter 5). This unity, which grows from, and at the same time supports social wellness will result in a more efficient and effective method to help meet the needs of others and follow the commands of the Bible.

"Red and yellow, black and white; they are precious in His sight; Jesus loves the little children of the world."

A simple children's song can remind us that Jesus loves all. We also need to remember that He created all. In addition to different personality types and skin colors, consider the different types of flowers, trees, dogs, cats, beetles, clouds, vegetables, birds and apples He made. Why did God create so many different things? Because, He delights in diversity. He also created all these things because He loves His children and He offers them to us as gifts to appreciate, respect and enjoy. Yet this diversity can be frightening to us because it makes us uncomfortable and uncertain. Diversity might mean we don't understand someone, and if we don't understand them, there is a possibility that we might not be able to predict or control them.

Rather, we should embrace and help people because they need God. This is a need of all people regardless of skin color, income level, denomination, political affiliation or ethnicity. We are all sinners in need of a savior, that savior is Jesus. This one fact unites us all.

What does Social Wellness look like?

Social wellness is more than just getting together over coffee or attending a party, it involves each person taking responsibility for, and contributing to their close personal relationships as well as their extended relationships in their community. Social wellness allows for healthy interdependence with others, this helps with our pursuit of harmony in our immediate and distant relationships. It involves developing and building close friendships by practicing empathy and effective listening. Social wellness also includes our caring for others while also allowing others to care for us.

It might sound contradictory but in many cases the person who thinks they are helping another person is actually being helped themselves. This can be compared to the practice of mentoring. The practice of mentoring is widely used because it is an effective way to evoke change and help others. It is especially beneficial because it not only benefits those who are being mentored but it also benefits those who are doing the mentoring.

By humbling ourselves and admitting we sometimes need help, and allowing others to help us, we not only help ourselves but we can also help the person we allow to help us. Jesus asked for assistance and He also allowed the nurturing, adoration and generosity of others. In Matthew 26: 36-46, we see Him telling His disciples to stay and watch with Him. In John 4:7-15, Jesus asked for a drink from a Samaritan woman at the well. There are also three references in the Bible; Matthew 26:7, Mark 14: 3, and John 12:3, to Jesus being anointed with expensive perfume.

All of these accounts of Jesus appear to either be a request for something or a display of His graciously receiving a person's offering of humbleness and generosity. Did He need any of these things? NO! He asked and allowed others to help Him for the good of those He made the request of.

—His request of water from the woman at the well was actually an offer; His gift of water that ends all thirst.

—Jesus' apparent need of the disciples when he called them to Gethsemane to watch and pray was not for His benefit, but to help them. Matthew 26:41, "Watch and pray lest you enter into temptation. The spirit is indeed willing, but the flesh is weak." He was displaying through His perfect example that He knew we would face fleshly difficulties and that we would have to submit to God and watch and pray to avoid entering into temptation.

—The anointing of Jesus appeared to some to be overly extravagant. It was typically used to coronate a king or for the installing of a priest. By anointing Jesus the women were acknowledging that He was both of these. Jesus allowing this confirmed His identity and also showed that He accepted their gifts and worship. This act of Jesus graciousness helped the women's Spiritual growth.

The gold standard for social wellness

Look at the life of Jesus and you will see complete and perfect social wellness. Everything He said and did was for the good of others. His life on this earth changed history. Remember what Jesus did first. He willingly took on the physical limitations of flesh, became a man and He hung out with people. "And the Word became flesh and dwelt among us" (John 1:14). Jesus didn't speak, or heal from a distance; He didn't sit in a majestic court with bodyguards keeping the commoners away from him. Jesus walked, talked and ate with …sinners. All of us fit into this category.

He lived a flawless life so that people could ultimately come into an intimate and trusting relationship with their Creator and experience wholeness. While walking this earth He met people where they were; He didn't just sit back and wait for them to come to Him.

A few days ago I heard someone talking about where they were <u>going</u> fishing. Fishermen <u>go</u> where the fish are. Those who have been called of Christ are to be fishers of men. That means <u>go</u> to people and meet them where they are at. I like a statement I heard an evangelist make "You have to catch 'em before you can clean 'em." This is what Jesus did. He died for us while we were still sinners. Thank God that He loved us first and sent His son to die for us. He did this for us first, because if He waited for us to get right before He saved us, it would never happen and we would never know Him. Jesus knew that without Him, forgiveness, wholeness, healing and eternal life were not possible for His creation.

While living in these physical bodies, we humans can never be the perfect example of social wellness as Jesus was because of our selfishness, fleshly desires, weakness, fears and limitations. As hard as we try we can never be totally Christ-like, while in this world. One of the glaring differences between Jesus and humans is that He doesn't need us, or anything for that matter. He is all knowing, all powerful, all loving and unlimited by anyone or anything.

God knows His creation better than we know ourselves and He uses us to be His voice, hands and feet to a lost world. God knows that we all have a need for a purpose and dream higher than our own personal self. We are also never more like Christ than when we show love and extend a hand of compassion to a lost and struggling person.

This is beautifully expressed in the poem below, by Teresa of Avila (1515-1582)

Christ Has No Body

Christ has no body but yours,

No hands, no feet on earth but yours,

Yours are the eyes with which He looks

Compassion on this world,

Yours are the feet with which He walks to do good,

Yours are the hands, with which He blesses all the world.

Yours are the hands, yours are the feet,

Yours are the eyes, you are His body.

Christ has no body now but yours,

No hands, no feet on earth but yours,

Yours are the eyes with which He looks

with compassion on this world.

Christ has no body now on earth but yours.

What social wellness looks like in daily life

—Acknowledge that it is better to contribute to the common welfare of the community and others rather than to think only of ourselves. "Even as I try to please everybody in everyway, for I am not seeking my own good, but for the good of many, so that they may be saved" (I Corinthians 10:33). If you are a Star Trek fan, you might remember Mr. Spock saying "The needs of the many outweigh the needs of the few or the one." That was pretty insightful for a Vulcan.

—Learn to balance your own needs with the needs of others "Let each of you look out not only for his own interest, but also for the interests of others" (Philippians 2:4). This verse acknowledges that we all have personal needs and weaknesses we are to look out for. It is good for us to allow ourselves to sometimes, be vulnerable and transparent to others and allow them to help us, it can actually help them. Our pride and desire to impress others can make people feel inadequate and rejected. It is okay to need help and to allow others to help you . We in return need to be ready to help them when needed.

—It is much better to live in harmony with others and our environment than to live in conflict with them. "Therefore, whatever you want men to do to you, do also to them, for this is the Law and the Prophets" (Matthew 7:12). Stop and really think about how peaceful and resourceful our communities would be if every member of our society would apply this verse into their personal lives on a daily basis. We can't control others, but we can control how we respond to situations and others. This is called personal accountability, which is imperative in every area of wholeness. We know that our choices affect our own personal wellbeing, our choices can also affect those we come in contact with.

—When possible, contribute time or money to social and community projects. There are tremendous needs all around us. But, regardless of the need, Jesus is the answer and He uses His saints to show that He is the answer to a hurting world. Christians have been so blessed because we have God in our lives. Now we are to share that blessing. This sharing may manifest itself in a financial gift that helps a missionary, or digs a well for the drought covered areas of Africa. It might be taking the time to tell a wounded person about the healing power of Jesus' blood. Another way to contribute your time might be a willingness to listen to someone who is going through a divorce or who has just lost a loved one.

—Exhibit kindness and justice when dealing with people "What does the Lord require of you, but to do justly, to love mercy and to walk humbly with your God?" (Micah 6:8). Each of us wants justice in our society, unfortunately it is frequently crushed, and innocent people are exploited and unfairly condemned. God is asking us to be like Him in this verse. Just to reiterate a point previously made, every action and every word of Jesus was for the benefit of the World. Imagine what your community would be like if the fairness and justice of our Heavenly Father ruled.

—Make a conscious effort to learn about others who are different than you. Not only will this effort help them by showing them that you care enough to listen, it will help you learn more about people, which helps in leading them to Christ. "I have become all things to all men, that I might by all means save some" (I Corinthians 9:22).

Earlier in this chapter we determined that God loves variety; just looking at the marvelous creation of nature proves this. He also loves people. He loves those that we don't agree with, He loves those who make us angry, and He loves those who are living in sin....not their sin. When we take the time to get to know these people who Jesus loves, it shows these people that we care. By getting to know them and listening to their hurts, confusion, anger and fears we are better equipped to help meet their need. Because we know our Savior is the answer to all of life's hurts. Often times we are too busy trying to show people how much we know. "People don't care how much you know, until they know how much you care" (unknown).

—Make regular attempts to communicate with the people around you. Communication involves not only talking, but also listening. In fact, I think we have all heard; "God gave us two ears so we could listen twice as much as we talk". Along with listening and considering what others have to say, we as followers of Christ need to share because, we have the best news ever. We serve a Savior who lives, loves and answers our prayers. Our Savior died to pay the price for the sins of all. After listening, share the good news.

—Follow the laws and rules of society. The lost world is watching Christians. They want to see if Christians do what they claim to do or if they act, live and speak like the rest of the world.

The Bible tells us to follow the laws of the land. "Let every soul be subject to the governing authorities. For there is no authority except from God, and the authorities that exist are appointed by God" (Romans 13:1). I know this probably isn't a popular thing to say in light of how our government has mishandled financial issues but, we are also to pay our taxes. If we are confused or in doubt about this, look at the example of Jesus, He paid taxes, and told us to do the same "render therefore to Caesar the things that are Caesar's, and to God the things that are God's" (Matthew 22:21).

Our world seems to be rejecting the truth of God and governments are becoming corrupt and abusing their powers. As Christians, praying for our country's leaders is the most powerful thing we can do. We are told in I Timothy 2:1-3, "Therefore I exhort first of all that supplication, prayers, intercessions, and giving of thanks be made for all men, for kings and all who are in authority, that we may lead a quiet and peaceable life in all godliness and reverence. For this is good and acceptable in the sight of God our Savior."

—Show compassion and help others when you can. Our world is full of anger, fear and corruption and is in great need of hope and healing. Jesus showed compassion in a way that no one ever has or ever will. His blood is powerful enough to heal, save and encourage. He is calling all His children to show and tell this. Unfortunately many believers get busy with life....yes, it happens to all of us, and our compassion wanes.

In my very early years of working to open the shelter for the homeless and victims of abuse, I remember a pastor of mine preaching a sermon on compassion. The following statement he made really hit home, "The enemy of compassion is busyness." This is so true, if the devil can keep us tied up with, temporal and material things we don't have time to invest in eternal things, which are people.

—Support and help with family, neighborhood, work and social gatherings. Contributing to a gathering or event has the potential to makes us feel like we matter and it gives us something to plan and work towards—or a purpose. Each of us needs to be and can be contributors. This contribution results in a win-win situation. Our help can make the gathering or event run more smoothly and it gives us the opportunity to both use the gifts that God has given us and to witness to others involved. The major benefit; unity and fellowship help make us strong.

Each of the items listed above can be summed up by the Golden Rule found in Matthew 7:12 and Luke 6:31. "Therefore, whatever you want men to do to you, do also to them, for this is the Law and the Prophets." That verse is often quoted by believers and non-believers. The problem is that not many are adhering to it, in fact, that verse is often perverted and lived in the daily lives of many as; *do unto others like they have done to you.* The desire to get even is not conducive to healthy relationships.

We are in but are not to be of this world

Christians have a challenging position. While living in this world, adhering to the laws of the land, listening to biased media, working for companies that have questionable agendas, seeking fun and recreational activities and being kind to others; we are to maintain Godly character and display choices that glorify God. How do we do this?

We become imitators of Christ. "Therefore be imitators of God as dear children. And walk in love, as Christ also has loved us and given Himself for us, an offering and a sacrifice to God for a sweet smelling aroma" (Ephesians 5:1-2). While Jesus dwelt among us, He lived His life to provide a perfect example of how we are to live. As Christians, our greatest purpose is "To know Christ and, to make Him known." When we get to know Christ, we then can become imitators of Him. When we become imitators of Christ, we are making His glory known. Jesus was in this world, but He was not of this world.

The entire life of Jesus was, to do His father's will. This was based on eternal love for mankind and God's desire to be reconciled with His children forever. Jesus' life consistently displays acts, words and teachings for the benefit of His creation. Look at some examples found in the Bible.

The impact of Jesus on society

The life, death and resurrection of Jesus were the greatest and most powerful events to ever take place in the history of the universe. It is humanly impossible to understand all the implications and blessings resulting from these events.

While walking on the earth Jesus not only lived a perfect life of love and devotion, He also performed many miracles. Only thirty-seven are specifically recorded in the Bible. We know however, that He performed many more. John 21:25 informs us, "And there are also many other things that Jesus did which if they were written one by one, I suppose that even the world itself could not contain the books that would be written."

Why did He perform all these miracles? These miracles obviously helped meet the present needs of people, but more importantly, they were intended to help the people believe. This desired belief did not always happen due to the hardness of man's hearts. These miraculous acts of Jesus are just one more example of God's extravagant generosity towards His children. These miracles were provisions to help people with an essential component of eternal salvation, their belief.

Jesus knew each and every need of the people He encountered, not only did He know, His deep compassion and unconditional love caused Him to act. The miracles of Jesus all revolved around meeting the basic physical needs of people. Jesus addressed and met the tangible and physical needs of people to confirm that their needs were important to Him. I also believe He performed these miracles just because He loves His children so much and He loves to give to them.

Not only did Jesus specialize in miracles and blessings possible only through divine intervention, He simultaneously endured intense physical pain, discomfort, rejection, betrayal, mocking and hatred. He suffered these things not because of His mistakes, failures or weakness. He endured them and eventually died on our behalf.

Jesus gave His life for us, we should be willing to live our lives for Him. Our personal social wellness is to be manifested to the world by following the actions of Christ. It is to be used on God's behalf to draw His precious creation back into fellowship with Him.

Chapter 16

OUR OPPORTUNITY TO BE A LIGHT

Just pick-up a newspaper or watch the news. Stories of social problems abound. Our world has become a very sick and frightening place. Pain, suffering, starvation, murder and corruption are everyday terms. They are intense terms, but we hear them so much they have become common place. Bad news floods the media. The needs are tremendous and they are growing, in fact it can seem overwhelming, but it is helpful to keep in mind that, where there is great need there is great opportunity.

Two major current social problems

Research and books written on social problems line the shelves in our book stores. In fact you can find multiple books written on each social problem that people are now facing. As numerous as social problems are, I believe that a majority of them result first and mostly from divorce and the breakdown of the family as God designed. The next major destructive force in society is addictions; which frequently stem from broken families or problems in the family. These two issues are very effective tools the devil uses to destroy God's creations. These two social illnesses are so destructive because they hurt not just the active and willing participants, but they bring tremendous suffering and pain to many innocent people.

Damage through divorce

Although divorce is a private matter and usually considered a family problem, it results in tremendous social problems. Families are the foundation of our society. The family is to be a source of comfort, encouragement, acceptance and grounding. When families fall apart, individuals in our society suffer because these human needs are not being met. When we see families start to crack and crumble we see societies that are beginning to deteriorate. Marriage, which is the foundation for the family was the very first institution created, and it was beautifully created by God, and there is nothing that Satan loves more than to destroy God's creation.

The divorce rate in America is terribly high. This should come as no surprise because Satan lives to attempt to destroy what God created. Divorce is a very difficult event to go through. The effects of divorce can be confusing and painful to adults. These effects however, can be a tragic and life changing event for the innocent children. Their foundation is crumbling, because the two most important people in their lives are separating. Children are often faced with a new home, new school, new step-parent or new siblings. This is a heavy load to carry when a person is still young and growing and developing.

Take a look at some of the effects of divorce on children, reported by the Heritage Foundation:

- In the areas of government and citizenship, divorce is followed by increases in the rates of juvenile crime, abuse, neglect, and addiction.
- In education, divorce is followed by diminished learning capacities and less high school and college degree attainment.
- Children from divorced homes perform more poorly in reading, spelling, and math, and repeat a grade more frequently than do children from two-parent intact families.
- In the marketplace, divorce precedes reductions in household income and the lifetime accumulation of wealth by family members. For families that were not poor before a divorce, income can drop by as much as 40 percent.
- Children raised in intact families have higher earnings as adults than do children from other family structures.

- In the realm of spiritual development, divorce is followed by a drop in both worship and recourse to prayer.
- Divorce weakens the health of children and shortens their life spans. It increases the rates of behavioral, emotional, and psychiatric problems, including suicide.
- Divorce can permanently weaken the child's relationship with his or her parents and peers. It often leads to destructive ways of handling conflict, a diminished competency in relationships, the early loss of virginity, and a diminished sense of masculinity or femininity.
- Divorce leads to more acceptance of and frequency of cohabitation, higher expectations of divorce and rates of divorce as an adult and less desire to have children.

In addition to the personal damage divorce causes, it also causes tremendous damage to society. In his book, "Fathers, Marriage and Welfare Reform", Psychologist Wade Horn states that, among long-term prison inmates, 70 percent grew up without fathers, as did 60 percent of rapists and 75 percent of adolescents charged with murder.

According to a U.S. Census Bureau report, poverty rates and dependence upon government programs also increase in conjunction with rising divorce rates. 65% of the food stamp recipients and 40% of those receiving TANF. are single parent households. 60% of U.S. children with mother-only homes are impoverished.

God loves the family dearly. His love for and value of the family is clearly displayed in I Timothy 5:8, "But if anyone does not provide for his own, and especially for those of his household, he has denied the faith and is worse than an unbeliever." I don't think there is much room for confusion here. We are to provide for the needs of our families.

Since we know that God loves and created the family, we must also be aware that the devil hates and works diligently to crush this beautiful creation. Satan lives to steal, kill and destroy and he is the father of lies. He opposes everything God stands for or created, and he will stop at nothing to eliminate this precious institution. Satan knows that this beautiful institution is the foundation of society and the best way to destroy a society is to weaken and destroy its foundation. His tools are deceptive and very effective.

One highly destructive tool actually started out as a helpful and much needed program. In response to the great depression, the welfare program was made a reality by Franklin D. Roosevelt in 1935. This program has changed and grown and is now know as TANF. This stands for: Temporary Assistance to Needy Families. The first word and also the key word is temporary. Unfortunately, it has become a lifestyle for many, handed down by the generation before them.

In our society today it is being shockingly abused, and has grown to an unmanageable size. Many recipients of this government program have children out of wedlock in order to receive a government issued check. We now have men and young teen boys who abandon their family, or couples who refuse to marry because the government benefits will be reduced if they step up to God's expectations for marriage and parents. I wonder if these folks are aware of I Timothy 5:8? Maybe they think this verse doesn't apply to them…. Who was it that said "you get more of whatever you subsidize." Our government's policies are subsidizing programs contrary to God's design.

The TANF program which was originally designed to help meet people's basic needs has turned into a controlling oppression, an oppression that is depriving individuals of the opportunity to struggle and see that they can overcome their struggles. These programs also stand in the way of young married couples working together as a team to solve problems, raise children as a united entity and develop a budget to manage their own personal households.

The TANF program, which was once a help has become a major hindrance. It is a ceiling, and it is a low ceiling. It deprives individuals of dreaming and hoping. It stops them from learning to manage personal finances. Worst of all, it brainwashes people into thinking that the government is their provider. These recipients of government programs often don't take personal responsibility for their financial choices, because the government will buy their food, pay their rent, provide health insurance, medication and transportation to medical appointments, pay for college, electric, water and gas bills.

For participants in the welfare-to-work program the government will put gas in their cars, pay for automobile repairs and cover day care expenses. But there isn't a government program that will tuck children into bed at night, eat dinner with them and teach little boys how to be respectful young men, or take children to church and introduce them to their Heavenly Father.

God's design of a mother and father for a child is the best design. Fathers offer qualities that mothers don't and vice versa. Two fathers or two mothers are a perversion to God's original plan and this type of relationship is very harmful to children. One mother or one father alone cannot provide what a Godly mother and father together can provide. The further we get from God's original design the more social problems we have.

What can you do about divorce and broken families?

I realize this is probably obvious, but I must say it. Pray! Pray for married couples that are considering divorce. Pray for young couples trying to build a family and are faced with financial burdens, pray for couples that might be dealing with life-threatening disease, pray for married men and women who are being tempted by members of the opposite sex. Pray for military couples who must live miles and miles away from each other. Pray that all married couples will learn to love and trust God and put him first. Pray that unwed couples who have children will unite in a God ordained marriage. God can change hearts and heal scars. He can deepen love and commitment.

God created marriage as a gift and help to His children, and he wants to see marriages that are thriving and lasting.

Another consideration for divorce help is your personal offering of support, friendship, guidance and encouragement to those who are in the process of or have already been through a divorce. Going through a divorce is a major event. It is life-changing and can shatter a person's dreams. It is an especially difficult experience for Christians as it can sometimes carry a great amount of shame, guilt and feelings of failure and inadequacy.

Many denominations look at divorce as a reason to avoid, criticize or demean others. This perception can keep hurting and broken people from the very place they need to be...the Church, fellowshipping with their brothers and sisters in Christ.

Instead of judging or possibly even rejecting those who have been divorced or those who are currently going through a divorce, we should be willing to listen to, comfort, encourage, accept and guide them during this difficult time. The church's willingness to do this is a way to offer practical help in their time of need and hurt. A benefit that can easily be overlooked when helping people through divorce is that their children are helped. A good way to help a child is to help their parents heal and grow so they as parents can better care for and nurture their children.

Helping adults and children find and look to Jesus though the pain and uncertainty of divorce is the best and most complete way we can help. When we help others we are reminded of how good God is because, we get the opportunity to see Him work and restore. Just one more example of how we are blessed ourselves by being willing to help others.

The famous author Stephen Covey wrote the book, *Seven Habits of Highly Effective People*. He then wrote a sequel to it called, *The 8th Habit: From Effectiveness to Greatness*. In this book, Mr. Covey stressed the importance of inspiring others to find their voice and also the using of our own voices to wisely serve others.

This is just a reiteration of how the mentoring process is so effective, both the mentor and the mentee are helped. Social wellness is a way of helping others find not only their voice, but of finding and accepting God, who created them, died for them and loves them unconditionally.

There is a beautiful and very touching song by Greg Long. It is called, "Help Somebody Cry". The chorus says, "Help somebody cry, be there for their tears. God will use your life to show that he is real." Our struggles, battles and even failures can be used by God. His word makes this promise to us in Romans 8:28 "We know that all things work together for good to those who love God, to those who are the called according to his purpose." This doesn't mean all things that happen are good, obviously, but it does mean that because God loves us so much and because He is so wise and so powerful, that He can bring a treasure out of our shame and torment. This verse is being repeated because I believe it would benefit everyone to make it part of their armor.

Our world is hurting, lost, confused, deceived, angry and frightened. We know the answer, Jesus. Now is the time His truth must be shared.

Addictions

The definition of addiction is: The state of being enslaved to a habit or practice or to something that is psychologically or physically habit-forming.

Addictions attach to and enslave a person's energy and desires to certain things, people, feelings or behaviors. These objects of attachment then become preoccupations and obsessions; they come to rule and ruin the lives of many. Does the word idolatry come to mind?

Addictions cause major problems in our world and have astronomically high financial ramifications. Addictions however are not at their heart social or financial problems. They originate from spiritual problems. If we truly desire to see people break away from the bondage of a life-controlling addiction, our methods of recovery must include God.

Some of the social problems caused by addictions include: high crime rates, break-up of the family, child abuse or negligence. In fact, alcohol or drug use is indicated in the majority of all child abuse cases and most violent offenders have a history of addiction. Addictions also negatively impact the individual's mental, physical, social and financial health. Keep in mind that our society is made up of individuals and high numbers of individuals dealing with addictions results in high numbers of social problems.

Addictions do not just involve the obvious; drugs, alcohol and gambling, addictions can occur with something seemingly good. The definition above describes addiction as being enslaved to. Any object, event or person that we become overly dependent on has the ability to enslave us and steal our peace, freedom and dreams.

"There is a God shaped vacuum in the heart of every man which cannot be filled by any created thing, but only by God, the creator, made known through Jesus." Blaise Pascal June 19, 1623-August 19, 1662.

Our human attempts to fill this God shaped vacuum may provide immediate short term pleasure but they eventually lead to unfulfillment, enslavement and possibly death. An addicted person lives according to the lie that if they just get more, they will be satisfied...but more is never enough.

What can the body of Christ do about addictions?

Some of the items mentioned in helping with divorce support can also be useful with addiction support. It is important to remember however, divorce is legal and although it can be painful and devastating it is not *usually* as destructive or dangerous as some additions can be.

Working in the field of social services for over twenty years opened my eyes to the very real damage that addictions cause. These years also showed that when an addict is in need they will often stop at nothing to get their need met. This may include stealing, lying or having their children lie or steal for them. Some of the most heart-breaking memories I have are of precious little children who were prostituted out by their own mothers to pay for a parent's drug addiction.

When we, the body of Christ hear of addiction we can get a little pompous and disgusted that people would do such things. It is important for us to humbly keep in mind that nobody ever wants to become an alcoholic when they take that first drink, become addicted when they smoke their first crack, snort cocaine for the first time or look at that first pornographic magazine. No person dealing with morbid obesity thought that first cookie grandma gave them to help with a boo-boo would lead to an unhealthy dependence on food.

These acts all feel good and serve a useful purpose at first, then they *hook* people. In time the hook (addiction) is so deep it is embedded in a person's being. These addicted persons are great at being addicted/hooked because they have done it so long. They forget what true peace, joy and freedom feel like. As bad and costly as the addictions are, to the active addict it is frightening to imagine a life without it.

Loving Christians must not just tell, but also show these addicted individuals the love, forgiveness, deliverance and life that Jesus came to give. They must be told about the healing power of His blood. They need to be reassured that Jesus does love them and there is nothing they have done that is so bad that Jesus can't save and forgive them. A large majority of individuals dealing with addictions have heard about God, and many of these individual have been abused or shamed by the same people who profess to know God. The very thing they need most is often the thing they fear and run from the most.

I am not trying to find or give excuses for addictive behavior. It is no different than any other personal behavior. It is all about a person's choices and each and every one of us is responsible for our choices, but in those dealing with addictions their choice makers are often malfunctioning or completely broke. Their choices are based on lies. They need to be made known of the truth of God. Jesus promises this in John 8:32, "And you shall know the truth and the truth shall set you free."

Offering life to those dealing with addictions without losing your own

As much as we want to help someone dealing with an addiction, we can't get clean or stay clean for them and we must not enable or excuse addictive behavior. It is necessary that we hold people accountable for their choices. We however do not allow a child to be hurt or neglected in the name of holding a parent accountable for the parent's bad choices.

When attempting to help someone dealing with an addiction remember that selfishness and deceit are at the center. Addicted persons are wonderful at hiding, justifying and nurturing their addictions. Their addiction has become their life and their god. As previously stated, these people do not know how to operate outside of their addiction. They are experts in their field.

Addictions are very difficult to deal with, so never be ashamed to seek or refer the addicted person to professional help. Be willing to provide transportation or support for them. Provide child care for a single parent who needs to go into a rehabilitation program. When financially possible, support Christ centered treatment programs. If your schedule allows, volunteer at one of these programs and become a friend to one of the clients who feels they don't have a friend; best of all introduce them to a friend who will never leave them or forsake them. One note here; more than just telling them about Jesus....let them see Him in your actions and the way you treat them. Many people in treatment centers have heard about Jesus, but haven't seen Him.

In addictions as well as every other struggle people face, the power of prayer can't be stated or depended upon enough. Pray for people living in the prison of addiction. God can deliver them! Pray for the loved ones and innocent children who are affected by someone's addiction. Pray that we and our brothers and sisters in Christ would extend a hand of grace to them, as Jesus did to us.

I discussed the two social problems of divorce and addiction in detail because I believe that they are two of the most destructive social problems our country is facing because they destroy families, and also because it is very likely that all of us know someone who is dealing with or has dealt with one or both of these issues. I also point out these two social problems because of the massive hurt I have seen result from them in my many years in social services.

Social problems seem to be increasing all around us. This is the result of the people of this world pulling further from their Creator. The more people do this, the more all types of problems will increase. In addition to divorce and addictions the following problems are increasing in frequency in our world: abortion, crime, division, diseases, war, famines, droughts, corruption, racism, homelessness, abuse, human trafficking, poverty and…. politicians, oops, can I say that last one? America and the world are in need of the healing touch of Jesus.

Through the development of our social wellness, which starts with spiritual wellness, we as Christians can equip ourselves to better reach the lost world and let them know that with God there is truth, hope, love, forgiveness and eternal life.

We each have the power to make choices that will enhance our personal relationships, our community and ultimately the world. Many people repeat the quote "You can't change the world." Not true! If each and every believer would reach out and touch the life of a hurting or lost person we could change our world, because when we help a person and lead them to Jesus, we help everyone they come in contact with.

This takes a united effort in which every person is doing their part, and every believer is working to follow the commands of God.

Jesus changed the world and He was just one. He told us in John 14:12, "Most assuredly, I say unto you, he who believes in Me, the works that I do he will do also: and greater works than these he will do, because I go to my Father." You want social wellness? I wonder what the world would look like if Christians truly believed in and based everything we did on this promise from Jesus. Belief predicts behavior.

Wherever you go, there you are !

Start wherever YOU are. People are everywhere; there is no shortage of them, which means there is no shortage of problems or needs. Every person who is a follower of Jesus is commanded "Go therefore and make disciples of all the nations, baptizing them in the name of the Father and of the Son and of the Holy Spirit, teaching them to observe all things I have commanded you, and lo, I am with you always, even to the end of the age" (Matthew 28:19-20). This is another great verse to memorize and go to when you are questioning your purpose. If you look back to chapter 6, where the expectations of Christians are listed you will see that the expectations God has for His children typically revolve around people. The life of Jesus demonstrated this and He is the way to build social wellness.

Interconnection. Spiritual problems can lead to social, financial, mental/emotional and physical weakness or brokenness. Spiritual wellness is the foundation to help mend and heal the brokenness of our world.

Chapter 17

FINANCIAL WELLNESS
NOT
FINANCIAL WORSHIP

"There is nothing in the world so demoralizing as money"

Sophocles (496 BC–406 BC)

The above quote was made centuries ago yet clearly points to what we see everyday in our present world. If we look at the problems around us we can see that the majority of them have some basis in either the lack of or pursuit of money. Often times one person's lack of resources is the result of another person's intense love and pursuit of money. We can be sure of this because God tells us this in His Word. I Timothy 6:9-10, "But those who desire to be rich fall into temptation and a snare, and into many foolish and harmful lusts which drown men in destruction and perdition. For the love of money is the root of all kinds of evil, for which some have strayed from the faith in their greediness and pierced themselves through with many sorrows."

Those verses are full of so much wisdom, and they succinctly sum up the root cause of all the World's problems. I know we are discussing financial wellness in this chapter, but money, contrary to popular belief is not the problem. Money and other resources are gifts from God to help meet our needs. Unfortunately, humans do with money, like we do with any other gift that God gives us, we misuse and idolize it. So money is not inherently bad. The power, attention and affection we give to money is what causes problems.

People get hung up on the word money in verse 10, but there are three key words in 1 Timothy 6:9-10 to which we should pay special attention. They are: desire, love and strayed.

The first word is *desire*. Our human fleshly desires frequently cause our separation from God, and fuel our bad choices. Fleshly desires are those desires that run contrary to God's principles. They are based on a selfish drive to meet our own personal needs. These desires cause us to mistakenly look to things other than God to meet our needs.

Attempts to fill our lives with anything other than provisions from God will result in lack of some type. It is Human nature to strive for more when we *perceive* that we have a lack of some type or another. Perceive was emphasized because frequently, we have all we need but, our greed and emptiness drive us to seek more. Lies of the world cause many to believe that more is the answer; more money, more success, more popularity, more food, more clothes, a bigger house, a newer car, etc....More of everything, except God. Our desires for things cause problems when they surpass our desire for God. So, it is our <u>desire</u> to be rich that causes us to fall into temptation and a snare, and into many foolish and harmful lusts.

Notice the desire wasn't simply for money or sufficiency; it was a desire to be rich, to have an abundance of material resources that goes beyond what one needs. Admit it, we all, have, at one time or another desired to be rich. We have also probably said at least once in our lives, "If I were rich, I would buy this, go there, help this person, support that organization, etc..." Every one of us is enticed in some way by what money can provide. The key is, "Be content with such things as you have. For He Himself has said, "I will never leave you or forsake you"(Heb. 13:5).

No person and no thing in this world can make the above promise. There are some who make this claim, but none else can keep it. We see far too many people consumed by the desire for riches rather than a constant friend and a savior who will never leave them. The wisdom of Proverbs addresses this in 23:4-5, "Do not overwork to be rich; Because of your own understanding cease! Will you set your eyes on that which is not? For riches certainly make themselves wings; They fly away like an eagle toward heaven."

Another warning about our desires is found in James 1:13-14, "Let no one say when he is tempted, 'I am tempted by God'; for God cannot be tempted by evil, nor does He Himself tempt anyone. But each one is tempted when he is drawn away by his own desires." Our human desires are the catalyst in many tragedies. Look at James 4:1, "Where do wars and fights come from among you? Do they not come from your desires for pleasure that war in your members?"

Without Jesus in our hearts our desires will be selfish and harmful because they are based on the old sinful nature, but when we ask Christ into our lives we become new and our desires can change. The old desires might diminish immediately, if they do, consider yourself highly blessed. Typically however, it is a slow and sometimes difficult process of renewing our minds and changing our choices. It is learning about and knowing that we have a Heavenly Father who we can trust in because, He is good all the time. "Delight yourself also in the Lord, And He will give you the desires of your heart" (Psalm 37:4).

The second word to pay attention to in 1Timothy 6:9-10 is, *love.* Just as money is not the problem, but our desires; obviously love is not the problem. The problem is that we love money. So it is the love of money, not money itself that leads to numerous atrocities and injustices all around the world. Our society has come to desire and love money more than it loves people and God. Our hearts are becoming cold and many are being deceived by the father of lies. Ever wonder how he got that title? The devil is very effective at deceiving people. Being a believer doesn't keep the devil from trying to deceive us. We should however continually lean on the Bible for truth; so that we are not deceived by the devil and wrongly place our love or hopes in money.

This love of money leads us to pursue more of it. Thoughts of it can consume our minds, steal our time and energy and for what? "He who loves silver will not be satisfied with silver; nor he who loves abundance, with increase. This also is vanity" (Ecclesiastes 5:10). More money might mean more things, but more things mean more to take care of and keep up with. More money might mean more power, but more power means more responsibility.

The third word to consider is, *strayed*. We stray because we love money and falsely believe that money can meet all our needs or it might help us feel significant and provide a sense of security. Verse 10 of 1Timothy 6 says: *"some have strayed from their faith in their greediness"*. Human greediness can cause us to stray from the faith. Our faith must be in God, not money, men or ourselves.

Since money is our current medium of exchange it is obviously very important and necessary to provide for our basic needs. It can buy many of the creature comforts we all desire. It can help make life a little easier and less stressful. Money can buy the attention of others and entertainment. Money can also be used to help prevent or halt the suffering and misfortune of others. The fulfilling of the Great Commission is also dependent upon money, so that we may go into all the world.

Most of these features afforded by money are good and can be useful in our lives. The problem comes when they become our life rather than being part of our life. It is very easy to get distracted by the desire for the temporary joy things can provide. In time, the desire and love for or trust in anything above God leads to: unfulfillment, bondage, lack, fear, confusion and weakness. The desire for the many promises of money consumes us and prevents us from filling our lives with what matters most. We must keep our focus on what is best not just what is good, that which is eternal, not temporal. God's wisdom, instruction and will are best. There is no amount of money, material possessions or power that will offer what a personal relationship with Jesus offers.

This is another <u>interconnection</u>: When we seek and obey the truths, commandments and promises of God (spiritual wellness) and set our mind on God's word (mental wellness), He will change our hearts and desires (mental, physical, financial, social and emotional wellness). God develops our wholeness by conforming us to the image of His son. Romans 8:29 asserts, "For whom He foreknew, He also predestined to be conformed to the image of His Son, that He might be the firstborn among many brethren." When the followers of Jesus conform to His image, we are better money managers.

The simplicity of Financial wellness

This chapter on financial wellness could in all practicality be the shortest chapter of the book. It could be summed up in one phrase: spend less than you make. It is a mathematical principle, if you don't have it, don't spend it. Yet, if it is so simple why are so many people dealing with money problems?

To me financial management is much like weight management, they both revolve around achieving and maintaining balance, a simple principle to know, but difficult to follow. With food we need to spend (or burn) more than we take in, with money the opposite is true; we need to take in more than we spend. However, for some reason that logic is not easy to put into practice in our daily lives.

Both food and money are good and necessary, and they are gifts from God, yet either or both of them have probably caused us all problems at one time in our lives. I believe this boils down to the unconscious and untrue belief that happiness, acceptance, protection, love, nurturance, approval and security can be found in food and/or money. Those needs are common to all people and they can be met on occasion by food or money, but only on a temporary basis.

Simply put financial management can be broken down into three actions: give a little, save a little and spend a little.

First, give a little. God asks for only a little from our increase, a tithe. This is a very small amount considering that everything we have is from God. In our uncertain economic times giving first seems almost counterintuitive, but we are told in Proverbs 3:9, "Honor God with your possessions, and with the firstfruits of all your increase." When we give to God first, before we pay our bills, go out to eat or go shopping we are honoring Him. We are showing that we trust Him to provide for all of our other needs. By first giving to Him it displays that He is most important in our life and we trust Him to meet our needs.

There is no doubt that Christians are to give. Jesus, the ultimate giver and the ultimate example of how we are to live, is quoted at the end of Acts 20:35, "that it is more blessed to give than to receive." Can you think of anyone in the history of the earth more qualified to make that statement? Since Jesus spoke that truth we would be wise to practice it!

Save a little. Why should Christians save? Some Bible verses seem to say that we shouldn't save; Luke 12:24, Matthew 6:19-21 and Luke 12:16-21. Other Bible verses seem to speak positively about saving and consider it wise. Proverbs 6:6-8, 13:11, 13:22, 21:20, and Genesis 41:47-49. Which ones should we follow, which verses are correct? All the verses are correct, the key principle to pick-up is balance. Verses found in 1Timothy 6:17-19 describes the balance. We will get to that.

Not to save?

When considering the verses that seem to discourage saving, Luke 12:24, says: "Consider the ravens, for they neither sow nor reap, which have neither storehouse nor barn; and God feeds them. Of how much more value are you than the birds?" This verse is letting us know that God is our provider and He will take care of us. This verse is also telling us not to worry. To confirm this read Luke 12: 22-34. The point here is not to avoid or refrain from saving, but to realize that God is our provider, and we should trust Him for all things, and not have an anxious mind. One more consideration is found in verse 33. We can save and set things or money aside, but they can be stolen or destroyed in an instant. As faithful stewards it is important for us to make investments that will last for eternity.

Another scripture that seems to present saving as negative is found in Luke 12:16-21. This is the story about the rich man who yielded plentifully and pulled his barns down to build bigger ones to store his crops and goods. The saving this man planned on doing was not bad, but this rich fool didn't just save, he hoarded. The word enough was not in his vocabulary. The words: others, generosity, charity or God weren't either. This rich man focused on himself and his possessions.

Matthew 6:19-21, "Do not lay up for yourselves treasures on earth, where moth and rust destroy and where thieves break in and steal; but lay up for yourselves treasures in heaven, were neither moth nor rust destroys and where thieves do not break in and steal. For where your treasure is, there your heart will be also." The point here is that we shouldn't focus on amassing great wealth because it can be lost, instead we should use our financial blessings for purposes that are heavenly and eternal.

To save !

Saving does seem like a very logical and intelligent habit to practice. None of us knows when our vehicles will break down, a medical emergency will occur or if an act of nature may destroy our home. If we have funds set aside we have some resources to help repair our car, seek medical attention and rebuild our home. Saving is also wise because there will come a day when we retire and no longer bring a paycheck home. When we save we are planning ahead for unexpected expenses, and making sure that we have resources necessary to survive when we are no longer working.

The book of Proverbs offers several verses about saving or planning. In chapter 6:6-8, we are told to go to the ant and consider her ways. The ant provides an example of hard work and planning. Proverbs 10:5 tells us, "He who gathers in summer is a wise son' He who sleeps in harvest is a son who causes shame."

Another affirmation to save is given in Proverbs 13:22, "A good man leaves an inheritance to his children's children, But the wealth of the sinner is stored up for the righteous." We can also read in Genesis 41:47-57, about Joseph and how his saving from the seven plentiful years was used to bless and save the land of Egypt from the severe famine.

Balance

1 Timothy 6:17-19, "Command those who are rich in this present age not to be haughty, nor to trust in uncertain riches but in the living God who gives us richly all things to enjoy. Let them do good, that they be rich in goods works, ready to give, willing to share, storing up for themselves a good foundation for the time to come, that they may lay hold on eternal life."

Those verses perfectly describe the attitude we should have towards our finances.

—We are to trust in God, not uncertain riches.

—We are to do good and share.

—Our sharing helps us store up a good foundation that will last for eternity.

Spend a little. Most people don't have any trouble *spending* money; it's the *little* part that gets them. When deciding what to buy and whether we spend large amounts of money or very little, we know that all our resources are God's. The way we choose to spend our money, after we tithe and save, is a reflection of what is important to us.

Housing, food, transportation expense, clothing and medical expenses are all facts of life. Living in this world requires all of them.

However the type and cost of these things is within our control. When we purchase something that is beyond our current income or something that is unnecessary or extravagant, we say with our purchase that the item is important to us. That purchase may require extra hours at work, which means time away from our family, or no time for exercise and proper sleep. Possibly we could manage the purchase by tightening up in others areas. Unfortunately, and too frequently, we are seeing these purchases equating to huge credit card debt.

Before making a purchase we need to ask ourselves the following questions:

1. Is this a need or simply a want?
2. Do, I have the money right now to buy this?
3. Will I enjoy this as much when the bill comes in as I am right now?
4. Does the company I am purchasing this from produce or derive profit from anything objectionable to the Bible?
5. Is this purchase going to enhance the quality of life for my family and me?
6. Can this purchase help create loving memories for my family?
7. Will this purchase require large amounts of time for maintenance?
8. Will the maintenance, storing, or cleaning of this purchase take time away from other more important issues?
9. Is this purchase merely for social recognition?
10. Do I need what I am buying, or is there actually a need for something else in my life?

If we will slow down and think through the previous questions, we can make wiser purchases. The process of thinking and asking ourselves these and other questions can help prevent impulsive spending.

Financial wellness is our looking to and obeying God's commandments in regards to His many provisions. We can trust God for all of our needs, this includes money.

God is the supplier of all. Philippians 4:19

He is the giver of every good and every perfect gift. James 1:17

He is the one, who gives us the power to get wealth. Deuteronomy 8:18

He is the Lord, Who has pleasure in the prosperity of His servants. Psalm 35:27

The Holy one of Israel, the Lord your God teaches you to profit. Isaiah 48:17

God can help manage your money, so your money doesn't manage you

Chapter 18

SPIRITUAL WELLNESS, BEING RIGHT WITH GOD

I have saved the best or most important component of wholeness for the last. Spiritual wellness is the best and most important because it is the foundation upon which all other components of our wholeness must stand, and the food from which they must be fed. "But the natural man does not receive the things of the Spirit of God, for they are foolishness to him; nor can he know them because they are spiritually discerned" (1 Corinthians 2:14). Spiritual wellness is imperative for us to discern the things of the Spirit of God.

Spiritual wellness is so powerful, immeasurable and essential in the life of a believer that quite honestly, I feel inadequate to write about it. I don't have a PhD in theology, or in any subject for that matter. I am not a Bible scholar, nor am I qualified to be a pastor. I truly identify with the words Paul penned in 1 Corinthians 2:1-5, "And, I brethren, when I came to you did not come with excellence of speech or of wisdom declaring to you the testimony of God. For I determined not to know anything among you except Jesus Christ and Him crucified. I was with you in weakness, in fear, and in much trembling. And my speech and my preaching were not with persuasive words of human wisdom, but in demonstration of the Spirit and of power, that your faith should not be in the wisdom of men but in the power of God." I know, and God knows that I know, I am not worthy or wise enough to write on my own or to fully explain spiritual wellness. It is only through His power that I can write!

I certainly am not good, holy or righteous of myself, but thanks to Jesus' indescribable gift I know Jesus! And I have been made the righteousness of Christ. I foolishly squandered many years directing my life myself, leaning on and looking to the ways of the world. The world's ways do not work. God always works! When we are tired He gives rest. When we are weak He is our strength. When we are ready to give up, God is our hope. When we are confounded by foolishness, He is our wisdom. When doubts and fears cloud our minds, God provides faith. Financial worries are extinguished by His provisions. In times of anxiousness, He gives peace. There is nothing that God can't do. He is complete, He is our sufficiency. Nothing else compares.

Where do we start?

God is too big to be explained in a chapter or two, or a whole book or whole libraries of books. The human mind can't fully comprehend God, or appreciate His goodness, and the human vocabulary is inadequate to provide sufficient words to explain our Creator.

Please allow me to humbly start with Genesis 1:1, "In the beginning God created the heavens and the earth." Not only did God create the heavens and earth, He created everything that exists between heaven and earth. "For by Him all things were created that are in heaven and that are on earth, visible and invisible, whether thrones or dominions or principalities or powers. All things were created through Him and for Him. And He is before all things, and in Him all things consist" (Colossians 1:16-17).

Knowing that God created all things, we know that He created us, and because of this we can know that He is the perfect source of information for questions and concerns about all things pertaining to our lives and our eternity. "But God has revealed them to us through His Spirit. For the Spirit searches all things, yes the deep things of God" (1 Corinthians 2:10).

When we need help, or something we own is in need of repair or replacement, we go to individuals who specialize in that particular field. If our automobiles aren't running correctly we call a mechanic, not our dentist. If our sink won't drain the plumber gets the call, not the pharmacy. Need a loan? Go to the bank, not the veterinarian. Specific problems require us to seek people with specific knowledge and training to help with these problems. Got problems with you? Call on God! Because He is our designer and creator, He knows us better than anyone, in fact He knows us better than we know ourselves. Take the time right now to get your Bible and read Psalm 139:1-17. If you can, read it out loud to yourself. You read it, right? After reading those verses can you think of anyone or anything more perfect or equipped to seek and trust in?

The world makes many false claims and empty promises, these falsehoods and vain promises transpire through the father of lies, Satan. This wicked and deceitful influence in our world doesn't want anyone to seek, know or fully trust and obey God. For if people would ask and receive God into their lives, and then completely trust in and wholly submit their entire life to Him, people could walk in victory. Remember though in order to enjoy victory, a battle has to be fought.

Spiritual victory means we see brothers and sisters in Christ living in and enjoying the abundant life Jesus came to give. Victory means believers can more easily develop unity and work together, to build the Kingdom of God. It also means peace and contentment during times of distress and struggle.

In an attempt to prevent this Satan continually lies and perverts God's word and promises. The devil works today the same way he did with Eve in the Garden of Eden, he continues to lie and deceive because it works so well. When we accept Jesus as the savior of our lives we have taken our first step toward defeating the lies of Satan. However, this is just the first step. Asking Jesus into our lives is not the end of the journey. It is just the beginning. This journey of development is not just for our prosperity and enjoyment; it is for the bigger calling of building God's kingdom.

With this in mind there are two questions we need to ask ourselves about our personal journey:

1. During my journey have I been helping anyone on their journey towards the wholeness that Jesus offers?

2. Will anyone come to know Jesus as their Savior through the course of my actions or words while I am on my journey?

As believers, our whole being and hope exists in God. The lost world needs to hear of this hope because, life is hard! Yes, I said that and I believe it. God is good, and.... life is hard! Life is doable for me only because I know that I serve a living God who loves me, who has a plan for me and who has promised to supply all my needs. He assured me in His word that he will never leave me or forsake me. He has also promised that He will make all things work for good, even my messes and foolish mistakes. But, what about life for those who have never came to this realization? When we do not tell a lost person about the God who loves them, died for them and wants to have a relationship with them and restore them, we are sinning. What is stopping us from telling others about this life changing promise?

We must all remember that every Christian is gifted in order to serve God. We have all been called to help build His kingdom so that the ministry of reconciliation can be fulfilled.

"Now all things are of God, who has reconciled us to Himself through Jesus Christ, and has given us the ministry of reconciliation, that is, that God was in Christ reconciling the world to Himself, not imputing their trespasses to them and has committed to us the word of reconciliation. Now then we are ambassadors for Christ, as though God were pleading through us; we implore you on Christ's behalf, be reconciled to God" (2 Corinthians 5:18-20).

Read those verses again and think about them for a minute. God wants us with Him. He wants US! How wonderful it is to know that the ruler of the universe wants to be with you and me. And, God is pleading through us to the lost world so that they may turn to Him. Why would a perfect and holy God want sinful man with Him, Because, God knows what we will become through His love. He looks beyond our past and what we are right now. If you ever doubt it, be encouraged by Philippians 1:6, "being confident of this very thing, that He who has begun a good work in you will complete *it* until the day of Jesus Christ". God loves and desires fellowship with His creation and God knows what He can do through and for His creation.

The important thing we need to remember about the gifts that God gives for the work of ministry is that they were *given* to us by our Heavenly Father. We did not earn them or work for them. These gifts are not given to use for self advancement or to take pride in, but to do His work. It is imperative for believers to keep in mind that the only good in us is Jesus, and this is a wonderful knowledge because, He is completely, 100 percent, abundantly enough for anything this world may throw at us. Whatever the problem, Jesus is the answer. Everything we are and everything that we have is because of our magnificent creator. Without God we would still be dust. Since God created man and the universe we live in, He is the complete source of truth, information, encouragement and instruction. God is never wrong!

I know that I take the many promises, blessings, the abundant forgiveness and grace that God has generously provided for granted. If we were to be honest, I think we will all agree that we are guilty of this to some degree. If we truly appreciated and understood how good God is and all He has done and is still doing for us, we would never complain, doubt, murmur, envy or criticize others. We would not be prideful but, rather we would humbly be thankful for and use the many gifts and resources He has given us on His behalf. I have recently discovered that at times I feel just a bit too good about myself and some of my "works" and I tend to forget, "For I know that in me (that is, in my flesh) nothing good dwells, for to will is present with me, but how to perform what is good I do not find" (Romans 7:18). All good things we possess are from <u>the</u> Greatest Giver.

Right now, are you saying to yourself? I already know all this. If so, are you putting it to use in your daily life at work, in your neighborhood, in class, on the bus or at the gym? The case could be that you know it, but don't genuinely trust it. Possibly you might even struggle with believing it. Remember when I previously asked; *if we say we believe something but we don't do it, do we really believe it?* And reconsider the statement: belief predicts behavior. How do we convince a world of the love, forgiveness and power that is available in Jesus Christ, if we ourselves are struggling with the total acceptance (belief) of everything that God has told us?

As previously stated, our own spiritual wellness is imperative for wholeness. In fact it is impossible to experience true wholeness without a relationship with God. Because we have a spirit, we are in need of spiritual wellness, this means we must feed, nurture and pay attention to our spiritual wellness, just as we would our physical wellness. Our bodies are an absolute essential to travel through this world and are very important, but without God they are just empty shells struggling to find fulfillment in the empty and fleeting promises of this world.

What's next?

Your Father is the ultimate ruler and the creator of all things. He is the King of all kings...and He loves you. He's got your back. Now you need to get to know Him. In order for us to intimately know God on a personal basis it is imperative that we spend time with Him and in His word. Unfortunately the artificially inflated cares of the world whittle this time away and we find that we spend more time and energy with our jobs, spouses, friends, hobbies, eating, exercising, studying, pets, gardens, automobiles, children, reading or watching ballgames. How long do you think your kids or pets would live, or how healthy do you think they would be if you showed them the same amount of attention, affection and time that you show God?

We feed our physical bodies everyday; hopefully we will start moving them on a regular basis. In addition to eating and possibly getting some type of physical activity on a daily basis we also sleep, drink water, watch television, take showers, send e-mails, talk on the phone and go to work everyday. Spending time with our Father should also be a daily activity. Time with Him is the best nourishment, guidance and encouragement available.

Spending time alone with God is like all other behaviors we engage in on a regular basis. Initially, it might be hard to find time, we might get distracted while we read the Bible, we might get drowsy while we pray, but the more we do it the better we get. The better we get, the more we enjoy it, the more we enjoy it, the more we do it. The more time we spend with God the more we can know Him, the more we know Him, the more we love and trust Him. When we love and trust Him, we want to obey Him. Our obedience leads us to know and do the will of our Father.

Do the most important things first

"Pray often, for prayer is a shield to the soul, a sacrifice to God, and a scourge for Satan." **John Bunyan (Nov. 1628 - Aug. 1688)**

My time with the Lord first thing in the morning is the favorite part of my day. I have come to this realization because I lived many years without it. The years with it are better beyond comparison. Now it is a habit. It is part of my lifestyle. It was difficult to get started at first because it required that I get up earlier so I could also get the kids off to school, get my work-out in and then make it to work on time. But you know what? I don't mind that at all now, in fact there are days when I wish I had gotten up earlier so I could have had more time alone to focus on, learn about, listen to and talk with Jesus. My time with God each day is my grounding, my comfort, and my encouragement. Getting to know my Heavenly Father is a joy that cannot be expressed.

Starting the day with Jesus is not only helpful for us; it is helpful for everyone we encounter that day. Our time alone with Jesus is so important that we need to make it the first thing we do, so that our time and energy doesn't get eaten up by our overloaded schedules. If we make it a priority and do it when we first get up we won't run out of time for God. Believe it or not, you will find that starting your day off with God will seem to provide more time and energy to accomplish what needs accomplishing. If we start our rising with God we won't bypass our time with Him if we happen to get consumed with our kid's activities or homework or if we happen to fall asleep watching television. We know we have the important stuff covered.

I realize that you know reading your Bible is important so, I am probably not offering you any new information. But knowing something and doing it are two different things. Many Christians do not have a daily quiet time alone with God. We must make it a priority, and when we do it opens the door to a deep and satisfying relationship with Him. It also helps arm us with truth so that we are ready to answer the many doubts and face the many cares of the world. "But sanctify the Lord God in your hearts, and always be ready to give a defense to everyone who asks you a reason for the hope that is in you, with meekness and fear" (1 Peter 3:15).

Interconnection—Time in God's word is foundational because it provides truth for us to base every component of our life upon.

Praise & Worship

These two acts help with our spiritual wellness because when we employ them we are being obedient, and our obedience to God turns out to be a blessing from God. Numerous verses tell us to praise the Lord. If we look to Psalm, which is a beautiful book of praise. We are all to praise God, "Let everything that has breath praise the Lord"

(Psalm 150:6). That verse includes you and me…because we breathe, which is possible only because of God.

We praise Him because, He is worthy of praise. "For the Lord is great and greatly to be praised: He is to be feared above all gods" (Psalm 96:4).

When we praise God we are turning our eyes upon Him. We are turning our minds upon Him. Our praise of God is an expression of our genuine heartfelt love, appreciation, honor and recognition of His awesome goodness, mighty power and His infinite majesty. Our time of praise is focused and centered on Him. With maturity, our lives should be the same. Praise helps us acknowledge and put God where He belongs; on the throne of our lives.

The New International Version (1984) of Psalm 22:3 best expresses this meaning. "Yet you are enthroned as the Holy one, You are the praise of Israel." This verse is stating a fact. God is THE Holy one and He is THE praise of Israel. Nothing changes that. Another version of that same verse is frequently quoted as, *"God inhabits the praises of His people".* This version seems to imply that our praises change God or bring Him down to our presence. This isn't the case because God is always with us and He never changes. We are the ones that move from Him and wrongfully give our loyalty and adoration to other things. We are the ones who need to deliberately set our minds and turn our hearts to God.

Praise and worship are such beautiful and satisfying times. It is like a comforting and encouraging medicine for our minds and souls. God likes and desires for us to engage in praise and worship, but we need it.

Praise helps prepare us for worship because we have recognized and put God where He belongs; on the throne. He is the ultimate Royalty of the universe and yet He loves us and died for us. Our only appropriate response is to approach Him in reverence and awe with total submission of all we have and all that we are. Both individual and corporate praise and worship are beneficial for our spiritual wellness.

<u>Interconnection</u>—Praise and worship improves our mental and emotional wellness. This affects all we do and say because everything begins with a thought.

Tithing & giving

The regular practice of tithing provides an avenue for God to reveal His incomprehensible generosity, and His creative and unexplainable accounting skills. It is truly amazing to see how God can take our measly offerings and gifts and multiply them to complete unimaginable missions. After we tithe it is also just as amazing to watch how He can take the remaining ninety percent of our income and stretch it to provide far beyond anything that we ourselves could stretch our 100 percent to provide. His math just doesn't work out on paper. When by faith we give back to God what is rightfully His to begin with, we will learn that He does truly meet all of our needs. We will also discover that we can never out give God.

Are you still struggling with tithing? Do your household finances still seem out of control? Look at Malachi 3:8-10, "Will a man rob God? Yet you have robbed Me! But you say in what way have we robbed You? In tithes and offerings. You are cursed with a curse for you have robbed Me, even this whole nation. Bring all the tithes into the storehouse, That there may be food in My house, And try me now in this, Says the Lord of hosts, If I will not open for you the windows of heaven and pour out for you such blessing that there will not be room enough to receive it."

When we do not tithe, not only are we robbing God, we are robbing ourselves from His intended blessings for us. Our disobedience leads to undesirable consequences in our lives and the lives of others because we are not being good stewards of the material blessings God has provided.

If we would trust God, because He is worthy of our trust, and obey what we are told in verse 10 we would see our financial struggling eventually come to an end. God challenges us to try Him. Tithing is a discipline and at first it is an act of faith, in time however, you will see it is just one more example of how God's commands are for our good. Our obedience in giving is one of the many ways God helps meet the needs and hurts of people all around the world. After seasons of giving and watching God pour out His blessing, you will wonder why some are so hesitant to tithe.

Interconnection—Being faithful in our giving is being obedient to God because we love and trust Him. This love and trust of our perfect Heavenly Father will strengthen our entire wellbeing. Our giving will be a blessing to us personally and will be used by God to help others.

Using your gift of service

It is difficult to see how using our gifts can help develop our personal spiritual wellness, because it actually seems like we are helping others when we are employing our gifts for God's purpose. Therein dwells the manifestation of God. We are never more like God than we are giving and serving.

This type of sacrificial using of our gifts, talents and resources on behalf of others is not normal for the natural man. It is through the moving of the Holy Spirit that we do this with a pure heart and pure intentions, not for the praise of men.

By using our God given gifts we can help others come to know Christ and find their place in His family. We can help nations overcome hunger and poverty. We can help people defeat their addictions, build their financial wellness, and heal from their emotional scars. Our gifts can also help others finally learn how to develop and enjoy fulfilling and Godly relations with others.

Interconnection—When we are willing to use our gifts for God, He strengthens and fortifies us for what ever area He has called us to. When we use our gifts for His work, we enjoy peace and rest in the nearness and fullness of God. When we work for and submit to Him we find our true purpose.

Fellowship with other believers

In the previous chapter on social wellness we identified in God's word that it is not good for man to be alone. Relationships are meant not only for the physical benefits of companionship and help with physical or financial needs, but also for our spiritual health.

Time with other believers helps offer us physical, audible and tangible support. Life in an ungodly world can bog us down, discourage us and steal our joy. Most of our days are spent in a world with values and beliefs that are hostile to the truths of God. Time with followers of Christ can offer encouragement and a time of renewal and strengthening. This time of fellowship can also provide a protection from temptation.

Fellowship also offers us a time to praise and worship God corporately. What a wonderful thing it is to bow down at the feet of our Master with others who have given their lives to Him. As we praise and worship Him, He is honored, glorified and exalted and we are nourished and drawn closer to Him and each other.

God loves to see His children enjoying, loving and encouraging each other because He loves us and He knows it is good for us.

Interconnection—Our spiritual wellness can be supported by spending time with our brothers and sisters in Christ. Fellowship with other believers can also help everyone's physical, mental, emotional and social wellness.

Giving thanks

Children of God have more to be thankful than can be comprehended. In fact it is impossible to fully express our gratitude for the multitude of blessings He has provided. When giving thanks it is normal to thank God for the good things in our lives and for the things we like. It is also easy to thank Him when situations work out the way we planned, but what about thanking Him for the things we don't like? We are meant to give thanks in all things. "In everything give thanks for this is the will of God in Christ Jesus for you" (1 Thessalonians 5:18). What if we thanked Him with a genuine heart for uncertain economic times, frightening medical diagnosis or for those difficult people or circumstances that frequently visit us?

Giving thanks in less than desirable situations acknowledges that we trust God in all things. It means that we know God is good when life is bad. When we thank Him during trying and uncomfortable times we are expressing our faith in His word and in His love for us. We can also give thanks in these times because trials allow us an opportunity to grow and develop a deeper trust in God.

Thanksgiving is a discipline or spiritual exercise that is necessary for a healthy soul. I am disappointed in myself because at times I still have to remind myself of all God has done for and given to me. What kind of numb minded selfish person could ever forget the many blessings of God? Someone like me…. Do you know anyone like that?

When we are down, experiencing envious or jealous thoughts, having a pity party or we are asking ourselves, "What's the use?" This is the time the discipline of giving thanks can help us break free from those thoughts and attitudes. It takes our minds off of ourselves and problems and puts them on God. Take time daily to thank God for everything, good and bad. The bad is an opportunity for God to reveal Himself to you in a new way.

"Enter into His gates with thanksgiving, and into His courts with praise. Be thankful to Him, and bless His name" (Psalm 100:4).

"Oh give thanks to the Lord for He is good! For His mercy endures forever" (Psalm 136:1).

"Giving thanks always for all things to God the Father in the name of our Lord Jesus Christ" (Ephesians 5:20).

"It is good to give thanks to the Lord, And to sing praises to Your name, O Most High" (Psalm 92:1).

Don't wait, stop and take a little time to give thanks right now.

Talk to God about it

Just as human relationships are built and strengthened by communication, so to is our relationship with God. The word prayer is frequently spoken about, but not frequently engaged in. Prayer is essential in our spiritual development. Numerous times throughout the Bible we are commanded to pray or seek God. Once more the generosity of God amazes me because He commands us to do this for our good. God doesn't need it. He knows how the stock market is standing, He knows the balance in your checking account and He knows what your temperature is right now. We don't need to enlighten God about anything.

Our time of prayer is a time to honestly share our thoughts, fears, sins, desires and pain. This is not a time to inform God of them because He already knows all about them, remember He was there before He brought you into this world. This time of transparency before God teaches us to be honest with ourselves. It is a time to be completely open and know that God hears us and loves us. It is a way He can reveal sin to us, encourage us, correct us or tenderly touch our hearts and bring a tear to our eye because He speaks to us so softly and personally when we open up to Him.

On this trip around the world each of us wears many hats and have many faces that we use for those around us. This is not something God intended for us to do, because sometimes we forget which one we are wearing. The numerous hats and faces we use become a load too difficult to manage and it gets distressing, confusing and tiring. Our time of open and honest prayer helps us look to God for His purposes and wisdom. It is a time of self education, and who better to educate us on ourselves than the One who made us?

One other need for prayer is our need for forgiveness. God tells that if we confess our sins He will forgive us. The confessing of our sins helps keep the lines of communication open with our Commander in Chief from above. The time of laying our sin before Him and asking His forgiveness is a time that we come into agreement with Him. We are saying, God, if you call it sin, I call it sin, and if you want it out of my life, I want it out of my life. We are confirming our need for Him and His forgiveness.

Just as we take showers to cleanse our physical bodies, we need prayer to cleanse our spirits. None of us would willingly go for two weeks without taking a shower, why would we wait two weeks to confess our sins?

Prayer and Bible reading are the meat and potatoes of our spiritual wellness. These two disciplines are personal and simple, yet absolutely essential and very powerful. Prayer is not just a means for our needs and the needs of others to be met, but it is a time to get alone with Jesus and get to know Him more.

Chapter 19

START LIVING IN THE VICTORY GOD GIVES

Not only has eternal life in heaven been secured for us through the blood of Jesus, but so has victory. We have been told of this many times in the Bible. Look at a few verses that confirm this:

"Now thanks be to God who always leads us in triumph in Christ, and through us diffuses the fragrance of His knowledge in every place" (2 Corinthians 2:14).

"But thanks be to God, who gives us the victory through our Lord Jesus Christ" (1 Corinthians 15:57).

"For whatever is born of God overcomes the world. And this is the victory that has overcome the world—our faith. Who is he who overcomes the world, but he who believes that Jesus is the Son of God" (1 John 5:4-5).

"Through God we will do valiantly, For it is He who shall tread down our enemies" (Psalm 108:13).

The key factor in the many Bible verses that speak of our victory and ability to overcome hinge upon one thing; our victory can be a reality only through Jesus, not ourselves. "I can do all things through Christ who strengthens me" (Philippians 4:13). The key words; *through Christ*.

Knowing that Jesus has paid the price and secured our victory, we must know that our ability to live in this victory is contingent upon two things, a song I grew up singing in church is titled by these two things. "Trust and Obey." The song goes on; "for there's no other way to be happy in Jesus but to trust and obey." Sounds pretty simple doesn't it. It is simple, but obviously simple doesn't always equal easy. Sounds like weight management, just take in less than you burn; or money management, spend less than you earn! Some of the simplest processes in life seem to be the hardest to follow. Maybe their simplicity is our downfall.

Think of the plan of salvation, it is simple and direct. It can't be earned and it is available to whosoever believes and calls upon the name of the Lord. Wow, is that really it? Just believe and then ask and receive? Yes, that's it, yet because of its simplicity untold millions have and will reject it. "But I fear, lest somehow, as the serpent deceived Eve by his craftiness, so your minds may be corrupted from the simplicity that is in Christ" (2 Corinthians 11:3). This came from Paul who feared the Corinthians would fall prey to the lies of Satan, as Eve did. This deceit would lead them away from their simple, single-minded devotion to Christ, to the error of religious rituals and false teachers.

We see the first stumbling block to our trust, deceit. One way Satan steals our joy, peace and victory is by causing us to doubt God. Our weapon to defeat the lies planted by Satan is the truth of God. It is imperative for believers to memorize scriptures. We must store them up so they are ready for use when we are under attack. Once we know the scriptures we must consciously and deliberately choose to believe them even in spite of uncertain physical circumstances. When our spouse is diagnosed with cancer we can say and choose to believe that God works all things for good for those who love Him. If your business has failed and you are months behind on your payments you must tell yourself and choose to believe that God shall supply all your needs.

You must truly trust that:

God loves you personally

God is all powerful

God knows all things

God has a good plan for your life

God provides for the sparrow, you are of more value than the sparrow

God provides forgiveness for all sin

God is in control

God's ways are not our ways

God's thoughts of you are more numerous than the sands of the seas

God delights in the prosperity of His servants

God is your strength, shield and provision

God sent the Holy Spirit to be your helper

God is the provider of every good and perfect gift

God loves people, all of us, and nothing can stop this

God has secured victory for His children

God works out our momentary afflictions for eternal glory

God cares about you, so you can cast your cares on Him

God started a good work in you when He came into your life,

God will complete it!

That is just a short list of the many things we can know and trust about God.

When we doubt God's love, we need to remind ourselves that He willingly died a brutal death for us. When we doubt his power or abilities, we need to remember that He created the earth and everything in it and performed the miracles in the Bible. When we doubt His presence we need to call to mind that He said He will never leave us or forsake us. God always keeps His word; although it sometimes takes a while. Even in this, we trust because we know His timing is perfect because He is perfect. Basically God has got it all covered. Sit back and look to Him. Take a deep breath and relax, God is still in control and nothing is too hard for Him. Learn this, believe this, and live by this.

Trusting God not only provides comfort, hope, encouragement and wisdom. It also helps us with our personal sins. Think about envy, where does it come from? It comes from the desire for something or some accomplishment that another has. When we trust that God has a good plan for our lives we can stop being envious.

What about speaking critically of others? There are two common motivators in this. First, we may feel a person has truly messed up and needs to be reprimanded. If it is not our job or responsibility to do this, and if we are not speaking to or about this person in a manner that pleases our Father we need to stop our critical talk immediately talk to God about it. He is the ultimate authority. He doesn't need us to criticize others.

Another reason we have a tendency to criticize others is in an attempt to help us feel better about ourselves. If, after some brutal self honesty, we find this describes our self, then we should tell our self that regardless of past mistakes, failures and current struggles God can and will use all of our messes. We can also take comfort in knowing that He is still working on us, and He will not stop until His will is fulfilled. Criticizing in no way brings us up, it only brings others down.

Another sin that could be eliminated by trusting in God is stealing. Maybe you don't steal money or rob anyone, but do you willfully neglect to tithe? Do you honestly report the time you spend at work? Does your expense report accurately represent where your money went? Do you fail to report all sources of income to avoid paying taxes? All of these behaviors reflect fear, a fear that God can't or won't meet your needs, so you have got to help Him out. If you trust that God will supply all your needs you won't need to be involved in any unscrupulous actions. When you trust God, you obey Him by: tithing, feeding the hungry, paying your taxes, being honest in all dealings and being a diligent worker. When we obey God He will bless us.

Consider addictions, which are a form of idolatry. We as humans have many needs, fears and desires. An addiction is a progressive development that starts initially by our own self-medication; a seeking of someone or something other than our Heavenly Father to meet our needs.

This approach may provide temporary relief or comfort but it leads to bondage or possibly worse. "Look all you who kindle a fire, who encircle yourselves with sparks; walk in the light of your fire and in the sparks you have kindled—This you shall have from My hand: you shall lie down in torment" (Isaiah 50:11).

What if we turned to God when someone wrongfully hurt us or lied to us, rather than seeking revenge? What if people leaned on God when they felt depressed or shameful about past sin instead of turning to alcohol or drugs? What if we trusted God for our prosperity rather than selling ourselves to our careers? How about seeking and allowing God's presence to satisfy us or even just accompany us through our lonely feelings, rather than turning to food or promiscuity? It seems so simple yet we all struggle with truly seeking and leaning wholly upon God, because we struggle to fully trust Him.

One final thought on addiction. We all deal with addictions in one form or another. Maybe not drugs, alcohol or gambling. But we are all addicted to sin. Don't believe it? Try to go one day without doing it. If you do possibly make it through the day and you recognize it, you probably took a little pride in yourself. There's that sin again.

When Jesus willingly gave His life and died on the cross, He paid the price for sin in full. His life, death and resurrection are the provision of righteousness and eternal life to those who believe and call upon Him. Our eternity was taken care of through the sacrifice of Jesus. Not only did He take care of eternity, Jesus also cares and offers help each day with our every step and with our every breath. He cares about every part of our lives while we are living in this present world.

Knowing that He cares and that He is with us always provides assurance of our victory. No, that doesn't mean we will always win, or that everything will turn out as we planned, but it means that no matter how terrible of an event we may encounter, God can and will use it for our good.

Our wholeness and victory is realized when we wait upon and fully trust in Him!

Before our Time is Over

I struggle with a conclusion because there is so much more that could be written and I don't want to leave out important information, yet at the same time I fear repeating myself. My genuine desire is to offer encouragement and hope by pointing to God and saying over and over He is the answer! I find that it is humanly impossible to completely mention all that God is, all that He has done and all that He can do.

My relationship with God and my knowledge and understanding of Him is just that, mine. How is your relationship with Him? What is your knowledge and understanding of God? Do you know Him deeply and personally? Do you desire time alone with Him? Do you truly trust Him with your deepest shame and desires? Do you rest in His comfort and strength when life spins out of control? If not, make a deliberate decision right now and ask Jesus to help you allow and seek Him to be your all. He can do it and He will do it, we are the ones getting in the way.

Much prayer went into this book and while completing this final section I want everyone reading it to know that I stopped and asked God to bless and strengthen each of you on your journey towards wholeness. He knows who will read this book and He knows every fear, pain, sin and hope that each of His children has because, He is The Way of Truth to a Life of Wholeness. Even though we are bringing our time together to an end, please know that you were brought before the Prince of Peace before you started reading. His will is for you to have an abundant life. I pray that this book will help you come to know this abundant life that

Jesus came to give. So, I end with a final verse for you to consider and trust in while living in this complex and often discouraging world.

"But as it is written: "Eye has not seen, nor ear heard, Nor have entered into the heart of man The things which God has prepared for those who love Him." I Corinthians 2:9

Join me, and be excited to see and know the things that God has prepared for us.

Notes

Chapter 3 : What is Wholeness?

Strong, J. *The exhaustive concordance of the bible, showing every word of the text of the common English version of the canonical books, and every occurrence of.* Peabody, MA: Hendrickson Pub, 2004. Print. (Strong)

MacArthur, John. *The MacArthur Study Bible.* Nashville: Thomas Nelson, 1997. John MacArthur, *The MacArthur Study Bible*, (Nashville: Thomas Nelson, 1997), 2566(MacArthur 1997)

MacArthur, John. *The MacArthur Study Bible.* Nashville: Thomas Nelson, 1997. John MacArthur, *The MacArthur Study Bible*, (Nashville: Thomas Nelson, 1997), 2688(MacArthur 1997)

Keller, Timothy. *Counterfeit Gods, The Empty Promises Of Money, Sex, And Power, And The Only Hope That Matters.* E P Dutton, 2010. Print.

Chapter 4: Seven Reasons Why Wholeness is Important

Chan, Francis, dir. *Just stop and think.* Prod. Matt Warren, Writ. Lori Morush, and Jim Morush. 2012. Web. 28 Feb 2013. <juststopandthink. com/stopthink-the-movie/>.

Chapter 5: The Eight reason Wholeness is Important

Introvigne, Massimo. *Christian Martyrs, one every five minutes:*<>. 35. Center for study of Global Christianity, 2011. Web. (Introvigne)

Chapter 7: The Physical Component of Wholeness

Rhode, Paul, Laura Ichikawa, Gregory Simon, Evette Ludman, Jennifer Linde, Robert Jeffery, and Belinds Operskalski. "Association of child sexual and physical abuse with obesity and depression in middle-aged women." *NIHPA Author Manuscripts.* 32.(2008):878–887. Print. ncbi.

nim.nih.gov/pmc/articles/PMC2609903 (Rhode, Ichikawa, Simon, Ludman, Linde, Jeffery, and Operskalski 878-887)

Chapter 8: The Value of Physical wellness

Floyd, Kimberly. "45 Million Dollar Body." *Ezinearticile.com*. 18 Jan. 2007: 1. Web. 24 Feb. 2013. <ezinearticles.com/?45-million-dollar-body&id=421953>(Floyd 1).

Kung, Hoyert. Center for Disease Control and Prevention. National Vital Statistics. *Deaths: Final Data for 2005*. 2008. Web. <cdc.gov/nchs/data/nvsr/nvsr56/nvsr5610.pdf>. (Kung Vol.56,Number10)

Admin, "5 Foods that affect your body like cocaine." *21cwoman.com*. 21cwoman, 03 Oct 2012. Web. 26 Feb 2013. <21cwoman.com/5-foods-that-affect-your-body-like-cocaine>(Admin).

Walker, Emily. "Health Insurers post record profits." *ABC News*. 12 Feb. 2010: n. page. Web. 25 Feb. 2013. <abcnews.go.com/health/healthcare/health-insurers-post-record-profits/story?id=9818699>. (Walker)

Mercola, Joseph. "Mercola.com." *I will not be pinkwashed*. N.p., 22 Feb. 2012. Web. 25 Feb 2013. <articles.mercola.com/sites/articles/archive/2012/02/22/breast-cancer-awareness-(Mercola)

Parenthood, Planned. Planned Parenthood Federation of America. *Annual Service Report*. 1994. Web. <nrcl.org/abortion/ppprov.html (Parenthood C.5)

Chapter : 9 Knowledge Alone Does Not Equal Success

Begley, Sharon. "The Cost of Obesity." *HUFF POST HEALTHY LIVING*. 30 Apr 2012: n. page. Web. 28 Feb. 2013. <huffingtonpost.com/2012/04130/obesity-cost-dollars-cents_n_1463763.html>.

LaRosa, John. "U.S. weight loss market worth $60.9 Billion." *prweb.com*. Prweb online visibility from focus, 09 May 2011. Web. 28 Feb 2013. <prweb.com/release/2011/5/prweb8393658.htm> (LaRosa)

Chapter 10: Eating For Wellness

Klem, ML, RR Wing, and Mt. McGuire. "Study of individuals successful at long-term maintenence of substantial weight loss." *American Journal of Clinical nutirtion.* (1997): 66, 239-246. Print. Winget, L.

Chapter 13: Rest, Replenish and Renew

Harding, Anne. "How Lack of Sleep Hurts Your Health." *HUFF POST HEALTHY LIVING.* 14 Mar 2012: n. page. Web. 28 Feb. 2013. <huffingtonpost.com/2012/03/14/sleep-(Harding)

Chapter 14: Mental and Emotional Wellness, Accentuate the Positive

It's called work for a reason. London, England: Penguin, 2007. Print. (Winget)

Maxwell, J. C. *How successful people think, change your thinking, change your life.* 1ST ED. Center st, 2009. Print. (Maxwell)

Tracy, B. *Change your thinking, change your life, how to unlock your full potential for success and achievement.* Wiley, 2003. Print. (Tracy)

Sterling, Ron. "The five factors of Mental wellness." *mentalwellness.ws.* Dr. Ron Sterling, 10 Apr 2011. Web. 27 Feb 2013 (Sterling).

Contributor, "What Does The Bible Say about Emotions." N.p., Online Posting to *ehow.com.* Web. 28 Feb. 2013. <ehow.com/about_4572075_what-does-bible-say-emotions.hml> (Contributor)

Chapter 16: Our Opportunity To Be A Light

Fagan, Patrick. "The Map of the Family." The Impact of marriage & Divorce on Children. The Heritage Foundation. 13 May 2004. Address.

Horn, Wade. *Fathers, Marriage and Welfare Reform.* Indianapolis: Hudson Institute, 1997. Print. (Horn)

Commerce, Department. U.S. Department of Commerce. United States Census Bureau. *Poverty Main*. 2013. Print. <census.gov.hhes/www/poverty>.(Commerce)

Covey, S. *The eighth habit: From effectiveness to greatness*. New York: Free Press, 2004. 97, 292. Print. (Covey 97, 292) addiction. Dictionary.com. *The American Heritage® Science Dictionary*. Houghton Mifflin Company. http://dictionary.reference.com/browse/addiction (accessed: February 28, 2013).